21

OLD AGE IS
ANOTHER COUNTRY

Other books by Page Smith

The Rise of Industrial America

A New Age Now Begins:
A People's History of the American Revolution (2 volumes)

The Shaping of America:
A People's History of the Young Republic

The Nation Comes of Age:
A People's History of the Ante-Bellum Years

Trial by Fire:
A People's History of the Civil War and Reconstruction

The Rise of Industrial America:
A People's History of the Post-Reconstruction Era

America Enters the World:
A People's History of the Progressive Era and World War I

Redeeming the Time:
A People's History of the 1920's and the New Deal

The Historian and History

The Constitution: A Documentary and Narrative History

Daughters of the Promised Land:
Women in American History

John Adams

Jefferson: A Revealing Biography

OLD AGE IS ANOTHER COUNTRY
A TRAVELER'S GUIDE

BY PAGE SMITH

THE CROSSING PRESS
FREEDOM, CA 95019

Library of Congress Cataloging-in-Publication Data

Smith, Page.
    Old age is another country: a traveler's guide/ by Page Smith.
        p. cm.
    ISBN 0-89594-802-8—ISBN 0-89594-776-5 (pbk)
    1. Aged—United States—Social conditions. 2. Old age—United
States. 3. Aging—United States. 4. Retirement—United States. I. Title.
HQ1064.U5S5917 1995
305.26'0973--dc20   9520303
                                                            CIP

TABLE OF CONTENTS

FOREWORD

AMERICANS HAVE ALWAYS BEEN AMBIVALENT ABOUT OLD AGE. Perhaps ambivalent is not the word, perhaps the word is hostile. The new and the young have since the early years of the republic been preferred over the old. We were from the first a New World. The American Revolution was, after all, the work of young men as, indeed, was the Constitution. The constitution of the state of New York set the retirement age for judges in the higher courts at sixty; in Connecticut and Maine, it was seventy, prompting John Adams to write to Thomas Jefferson that he could "never forgive New York, Connecticut or Maine for turning out Venerable Men of sixty or seventy from the seats of Judgement, when their judgement is often the best." It was young men and young women, in the main, who pushed the frontier Westward. In some of the state and territorial legislatures the average age of members was in the early thirties.

So, in a certain sense, old men and women have, throughout our history, been regarded—with, of course, many notable exceptions—as irrelevant or, worse, a burden to be borne.

Such American attitudes toward age are strikingly different from those of more traditional societies where the old are respected and sometimes venerated for their wisdom, their accumulated experience. They are, in such societies, the elders and shamans, the custodians of the tribe's or clan's memories, the storytellers, the sages. In certain cultures, married children live in the home of the son's parents and live, moreover, in subordination to an often tyrannical matriarch. Under such circumstances old age is a privileged status, one to be anticipated and enjoyed. It brings with it authority and power. In the United States in A.D. 1995 it brings Social Security checks, nursing homes, retirement communities, golf, and cruises but little respect. The old are accepted for the economic or political power they may wield but not for the wisdom they may have accumulated during the course of a long life.

Take away wisdom, the very notion of it, and you rob the old of their silver and gold, intellectually and psychologically speaking. If to be old is not to be wise (granting of course that all the old are not always wise) then it is simply to be obsolete, like a discarded office machine or a worn-out tractor. All that is left is golf.

Obviously, we cannot solve this problem (which in my view goes right to the heart of many of the ills of our society) by a Congressional resolution or a Presidential edict declaring that the old are vessels of untapped wisdom. Untapped what? But we can make a modest beginning in learning what old age is.

Several years ago, a brash young sportscaster, interviewing Lou Holtz, then the coach of the Arkansas Razorbacks, on the occasion of his fiftieth birthday asked him how it felt to be so old. A poker-faced Holtz replied, "Considering the alternative, not so bad." Getting there is, at least in the minds of most people, better than not getting there, dismal as that may in many ways be. Indeed, it must be said as plainly as possible that getting old is a pain in the ass as well as in other parts of the anatomy. Yet, as I say, most people doggedly pursue that goal. In other words they want to live as long as possible.

A wise man (me) has noted that there are two common experiences in life so vivid and powerful that no one can prepare us for them—childbirth and old age. Old age comes upon us stealthily. An ache here, a pain there, the almost imperceptible diminution of some sense: sight or hearing perhaps most commonly. At the same time we have no internal clock. We do not perceive ourselves as old and we are startled to see it in the eyes or words of others. I recall the first time some insolent young whelp addressed me as "Gramps," as in "How are ya, Gramps?" I contemplated a sharp blow to the head as the only proper rejoinder but wisely (the result of years of experience) limited my reply to: "OK, sonny." Aches and pains aside, we do not feel old *inside*.

At the same time it must be confessed age changes one's perspective on virtually everything in the world: the various aspects of Time (its passage, most notably); day and night, especially night; food; sex; the material world; money; and so on.

In a real sense the world is divided into two major and mutually exclusive categories: the old and the not-old. Everyone from zero to what? fifty-five or sixty? is not-old. Everyone from fifty-five or sixty to eighty, ninety or, God forbid, one hundred is old (within "old" we now have a number of sub-categories: young old, frail old, old old). But my point is that the not-old, and among the not-old, especially the young, view the old as a great indiscriminate group. In some instances a young person's definition of old can be thoroughly unnerving. When I was a graduate student in my thirties, my wife and I had a precocious young friend named Saul Tauster who was a law student at the age of twenty-one. He kept telling us of this older couple he was anxious for us to meet. They had such a youthful attitude toward life. Despite their years they were young in spirit etc. Finally I asked, a bit apprehensively: how old were these paragons? Well, Tauster guessed, about thirty.

When an aunt of mine died many years ago I was surprised to hear her friends and relatives lament her death as untimely. She seemed very old to me. I later calculated that she was in her early fifties. That certainly seems untimely to me now.

Then there is the matter of generations, the disposition of the young and old in our society to live in very different worlds. The great American essayist, John Jay Chapman, noted that social intercourse between generations was the basis of any civilized society. When Sarah Whitman, the great Boston hostess, died, Chapman noted that mingling "old and young together" as she did in her entertaining, "is the first requisite of agreeable society, and the only way of civilizing the younger generation. Whenever the practice falls into disuse, the boys and girls will run to seed as they grow up. Young people are naturally barbarians and unless they are furnished with examples of good manners they soon become negligent, unashamed and illiterate.... They would forget reading and writing, history, clothes, the multiplication table and how to tell time, if they were entirely abandoned by their elders." To prevent the deterioration of the young is perhaps the principal justification for intergenerational social life, or society in the non-socialite sense of the word. It is also exemplary for the old who need someone to listen to them.

Now, of course, old people are the focus of attention by the media. Endless articles, documentaries, conferences, on and on ad nauseam and ad infinitum. We hear talk of ageism. Geriatrics is a burgeoning field. But the vast majority of the experts are in the category not-old and so have very little notion, beyond the merely statistical, of what they're talking about.

Old people now constitute a powerful force in local and national politics. We have one of the most powerful lobbies in Washington. If we can't have respect, we'll, by God, have money and other perquisites, whether we need them or not. We'll behave like any other special interest group, advancing our interests at the expense, if necessary, of other less powerful interests and since there are an enormous (and growing) number of us, we'll get our goodies and let the next generation pay for them.

Old is where most Americans, with a little luck, will spend most of their lives. If we break not-old into its traditional phases we get something like this: childhood, a period of, let us say, ten years (from 3 to 13); adolescence (also known as teenage), roughly five years, 13 to 18; youth (generally overlapping with adolescence), 18 to 35; middle age, 40 to 55 or 60 (in Japan the mandatory retirement age is 58); old age from 55 or 60 to death. Since the longevity of Americans is increasing at an alarming rate, it seems safe to assume that many Americans will or already are living into their late seventies (women, into their eighties). Thus Americans will be "old" longer than they will have been "young" or even "middle-aged." What these Americans will do with what have been called, with a classic American disposition to gloss over unpleasant realities, their "Golden Years," is of vast importance to them and to the future of this country.

"Old" means something very different to someone who dies at the age of sixty or thereabouts than to someone who lives to eighty-five or ninety. We all start at birth but we die at a wide range of ages even within the category "old." And we die early or late to some degree as a consequence of how we live, the work we do, the things we eat, and the places where we live. It is my basic assumption that growing old is a pain in the ass; at best, a mitigated disaster. For many Americans growing old is an *un*mitigated disaster. These are the economically marginal old, the old with too little money to maintain their dignity, the ailing old, not quite dead and not quite alive. The things that mitigate the disaster of old age are fairly obvious. Among the obviously mitigating circumstances first and undoubtedly most important of all, are a loving and attentive family, then friends (especially young friends), "interests," physical activity of some kind, and a reasonable degree of health, age considered.

Another mitigating circumstance is money; not lots of money but enough to live in some comfort and independence. If, for instance, you are old and ailing (and most of the old have *some* ailment or other—often quite a few) and have money to buy care, money to pay for someone capable and concerned to do those things you can no longer do for yourself, life is almost certain to be brighter than if, rated as impoverished, you are shunted off to a nursing home. And if, when increasing decrepitude makes it impossible for you to enjoy consolations of the familiar, you can afford to live in a well-ordered, church-run home, your last years will doubtless be less grim.

All these mitigations are chancy in the extreme and most of them are beyond the control of any particular old person although I suppose it could be argued that putting money by during one's productive years and having a large and affectionate family are measures within the capability of many individuals. Yet the sober fact is that numerous Americans, worthy in every way of a decent old age, lack the financial means to insure it, particularly in its latter stages.

In a sense, growing old means devising strategies for a campaign over unfamiliar territory where one has to improvise as one goes along. The last campaign, the final battle, is the most arduous, the most demanding, of all of life's challenges and the only one certain, no matter how bravely and resourcefully fought, to end in defeat.

The question thus becomes in its starkest terms how to minimize the pain and, as we have noted, mitigate the disaster. To pretend that one is not growing old, to run after youthful emblems, to affect a youthful life-style, is to augment the negatives. Nor do I believe in growing old "gracefully"; William Butler Yeats defiantly proclaimed his "lust and rage" at the encroachments of age. That seems to me a healthier response than "growing old gracefully." I'm not even sure what the phrase means (it brings to mind a series of creaky pirouettes; or perhaps a faded kind of gentility). Since it is my argument that growing old changes virtually every aspect of one's relationship to the world, it should be useful to contemplate the range and nature of these changes. Take the day and night, for example. Night in some ways becomes the most difficult and problematical part of existence for old people. Sometimes sleep is fitful, waking frequent, dreams strange and troubling.

One visits old haunts in dreams, encounters dead friends or parents, often experiences a piercing sense of loss; sometimes dreams are more pedestrian. I dream that I am searching desperately for some place to relieve myself. Everywhere I turn I find bathroom doors locked, toilets clogged or broken or located in public areas. These episodes usually occur, for reasons that I refuse to speculate about, at Harvard University where I pursued graduate studies many years ago without, so far as I can recall, having difficulty locating men's rooms.

We are, we oldsters, uncertain voyagers of the night. "How was it with you, last night?" I ask my wife when she wakes. "A good night? No bad dreams?"

By the same token, a day is very different for the old. For many, the day is, as the night, something to be gotten through. But the day is, after all, reasonably under one's own control. It can be laid out, planned and executed according to plan. Or allowed to unfold in its own way. A day is quite different in its rhythm for an old woman than for an old man. The old man is often habituated to a day measured out in activities needed to make a living, his job in short. He has experienced relatively little "unstructured time." Even on vacations he has been inclined to plan everything to the last detail and minute. Now (suddenly old, i.e. retired), the old man finds a day may turn into a dilemma. He has the vague feeling he may need a hobby. Perhaps he invests in a TV dish to increase the range of endurable TV programs and flirts with the notion of becoming a couch potato. He writes letters to old friends and to the local newspaper.

In some circles the old man and his wife begin a strange, rootless hegira around the country and sometimes around the world. They purchase a motor home or a travel cruiser and, often accompanied by friends, they start off in a mini-caravan to explore the "good old U.S. of A." One finds these aging travelers everywhere, following the seasons: Montana, Wyoming, Colorado in the summer, Florida or Arizona in the winter, California all year round. Nothing wrong with that surely, but it doesn't have much future and it automatically denies the travelers an established place in a familiar community. However, given the ambivalent position of the old in our society, it may be as good a solution as some and better than others.

But we were talking about a day in the life of an old man, less so of an old woman. There is certainly more than a little to the idea that an old man can rediscover days, let them run their courses full of casual and often unexpected pleasures, most of them having to do with the natural world. The day slows down for the old; different days have different moods or textures to them. Some of this variation is seasonal, some the consequence of learning to look, to "take time," to "loaf and invite the soul." I am tempted to argue that the first important exercise of a man when he becomes "old" is to grapple with that unit of time called "a day." When, for instance, to get up. When and what to eat for breakfast. For lunch. For dinner. How to spend the evening. When to go to bed.

Now all of this may seem frivolous or foolish but it is the essence of growing old. It lies at the heart of mitigating the disaster of growing old. A day should be mastered even before starting to play golf (golf is all right in its place but it should not become a substitute for existence).

To fail to master a day may well be to become "golf dependent," a truly desperate condition.

NAMING OLD AGE

OLD AGE VIEWED FROM THE OUTSIDE AND FROM THE INSIDE

LEON TROTSKY, OF ALL PEOPLE, SAID THAT THE BIGGEST SURPRISE that comes to a man (and, presumably a woman) is old age. Who would have thought that the old Bolshevik was so perceptive? It may have been his most astute observation.

I sometimes wonder if there is really any way to prepare those who are not yet old for what I would say is, on the whole, the quite disconcerting surprise of old age. You can't just go around collaring younger Americans and saying, "Look, kid, you're going to be what our society defines as 'old' someday, and someday sooner than you think and, boy, are you going to be surprised. Do you have a minute? Let me tell you what is in store for you so you won't be so surprised." Maybe being surprised by old age is inevitable: maybe it's just part of being old.

On the other hand perhaps a literary approach has something to be said for it. If the not-yet-old were to read novels, plays and short stories about old age, they might not go wandering into old age in such a state of bewilderment. Part of the problem is that, so far as I can discover, most of those who write stories, plays, etc. about old people or old age are, themselves, comparatively young. There are plenty of old writers of course, but by and large they don't seem much inclined to turn out fiction in which the principal characters are old.

I suppose the most famous old man in literature is King Lear, not to be sure a very cheering picture of old age. All this by way of introducing an anthology of "modern short stories on aging," entitled *Full Measure*. Edited by Dorothy Sennett with a foreword by Carol Bly, it seems to be designed to prevent those who work with old men and women from stereotyping old people. The editor and preface writer apparently have little hope that old people themselves will read stories of fictional old people (why should we, we're already there) and many of the stories are depressing enough. Sennett in her preface writes, "Although we survivors are vulnerable, we are tough. We may have lost a great deal, but we know that to survive we must hang on to something. We understand not only that life ends, but that it renews itself, and in renewal lies survival." She includes a quotation from Simone de Beauvoir: "…the whole meaning of our life is in the question [of] the future that is waiting for us. If we do not know what we are going to be, we cannot know what we are: let us recognize ourselves in this old man or that old woman."

The stories themselves run the gamut from tragic to hilarious. In "Leaving the Yellow House," a story by Saul Bellow, old Hattie, clinging to a lonely existence in her treasured yellow house in the desert, and to her battered old car which is her only link to the outside world, solacing herself with booze, is a classic survivor, a woman who toughs it out in the face of manifold afflictions. Carol Bly's story is of Harriet White, resident of an old folks' home, who makes a last gallant pilgrimage to her "real" home, a now-much-run-down farm soon to be torn down by a developer.

Several stories are about old professors or doctors. Joyce Carol Oates tells of an ancient philosophy professor whose friendship with an abused and battered child rescues him from the sterility of a world of increasingly convoluted thought. John Cheever's old professor laments the fact that he never won the Nobel Prize while fantasizing about sexual encounters. Cheever's story struck me as the most perceptive account of old men's preoccupation with the erotic, one of the "surprises" of old men's old age (about old women I know nothing). Much the same theme is carried on in Bernard Malamud's "In Retirement." Here the hero is a comparatively young (sixty-five) retired doctor who develops a consuming fantasy about a handsome young woman of apparently easy morals who lives in his apartment house. Gradually he convinces himself that she might welcome the attentions of an older man, mature and worldly wise, a kind of father/lover. He writes her a letter suggesting such a relationship and watches, hidden behind a potted palm in the lobby, as she reads it and tears it up contemptuously.

One of the most engaging tales is John Sayles's tale of the Anarchist's convention, a gathering of old anarchists who fought and bled in the tumultuous political battles of the 1920s and 1930s. When the manager of the hotel where they are meeting tries to move them to provide space for a Rotary Club dinner, they lock arms and begin to sing in cracked voices the old Wobbly song, "We Shall Not Be Moved."

V.S. Pritchett's "Tea with Mrs. Bittell," is an opposite sex companion piece to Malamud's story. Mrs. Bittell's longing for companionship makes her the victim of two predatory young men.

Well, this is not a book review. There are some twenty-three stories in the anthology and the question here addressed is the one we started with: is there an audience for short stories and novels about old men and old women—about, in short, old age? I confess to mixed feelings. If I had come across one or the other of these stories in some magazine or journal I would, I assume, have judged it on its own merit quite apart from the subject matter. Do I want to read a collection of short stories about nothing but old age? Since the great majority of them are written by authors who are not old, how much credence should I, or, indeed anyone else, give them as accurate pictures of the mysterious and surprising world of the old? And is that even a fair or relevant question? The intent of the authors was not primarily (or even secondarily) to inform us about the nature of old age. In any event, they don't really know much about it, not being old, but rather, like any writer of fiction, wanted to create a convincing realm of the imagination. In this respect some authors, of course, succeed better than others. As to whether they meet Carol Bly's expectation of breaking down the stereotypes of old people that many younger people have, I would have to say the jury is still out on that one. I suspect that they may do more to reinforce stereotypes than to destroy them. There are, after all, as many ways of being old as there are old people and as many surprises.

We now have, in practical fact, two literary genres dealing with old age. Besides writers of fiction who write about old characters, we have old people who write about old age. An example of the second category—writings by women and men who are themselves old and who are reflecting in a variety of literary forms on the nature and meaning of old age—came to hand in the past week. *Songs of Experience: An Anthology of Literature on Growing Old,* edited by Margaret C. Fowler and Priscilla McCutheon, I found enthralling. A number of contributors write of the way in which a deep sense of the beauty and power (and mysteriousness) of life has grown in them with the passage of the years.

Malcolm Cowley, the critic and contemporary of Hemingway, Faulkner and Fitzgerald, wrote *The View from 80.* "Even before he or she is 80, the aging person may undergo another identity crisis like that of adolescence....Now, when he looks in the mirror, he asks himself 'Is this really me?'....In his new makeup he is called upon to play a new role in a play that must be improvised." Cowley quotes "that long-lived man of letters," André Gide, who wrote: "My heart has remained so young that I have the continual feeling of playing a part, the part of the 70-year-old that I certainly am and the infirmities and weaknesses that remind me of my age act like a prompter, reminding me of my lines when I tend to stray." The same theme appears in any number of selections.

"I feel so young inside and yet my old body requires that I acquiesce in a role that life demands of us all." How often we simply forget that we are old until our muscles or our joints (or the expression on someone's face) remind us! This, I suspect, is especially hard for younger people to understand—the youthful spirit in the decaying body.

Another theme common to many of the writers is that we stumble or wander into old age without any real warning. M.F.K. Fisher, beautiful enough to break your heart when she was young, notes: "Parts of the aging process are scary, of course, but the more we know about them, the less they need be. That is why I wish we were more deliberately taught, in early years, to prepare for this condition." Another contributor, Polly Francis, touches the same chord: "Age creeps up so stealthily that it is often with a shock that we become aware of its presence. Perhaps that is why so many of us reach old age utterly unprepared to meet its demands." Fisher does not mean "taught" in any academic sense. The only way we can be "taught" about old age, as she herself notes, is by living with and experiencing old age in those we love, grandparents most typically but by no means exclusively. In Fisher's view it is "Our housing [that] is to blame." Most of us live in houses too small to contain those older members of a family—grandparents or elderly aunts—who used to be an essential part of the so-called "extended family." Beyond that we value our "freedom" and our "independence" too much to endure the small (and not so small) accommodations that intergenerational living requires. Ironically, at the same time we run after every kind of support group that promises to remedy our cosmic loneliness. Someone who can't bear the thought of living with an older (or younger) relative will be tireless in searching out a pseudo-family that shares his/her particular despair. "Yes," Fisher concedes, "housing is to blame. Children and old people and the parents in between should be able to live together, in order to learn how to die with grace, together."

Well, no, I would respectfully disagree. It is not the housing that is the problem (although that certainly is part of it); it is a failure of imagination and of heart.

The poet, John Hall Wheelock, in his "Song on Reaching Seventy" writes of the thrush that defies the "menacing night," adding: "Oh, now / Before the coming of a greater night / How bitterly sweet and dear / All things have grown." The general tone of his poem is that of the imminence of death. The image of the "gathering dark" is stressed. One can hardly resist pointing out that Wheelock lived another twenty-two years, dying when he was ninety-two. That simple fact reminds us of one of the most disconcerting aspects of old age: the fact that we usually haven't the vaguest notion of when it will end or how. Here was John Wheelock all geared up to exit shortly. What did he think when he found out that he was fated to hang around for two more decades? Did he cheer up and stop worrying about the "menacing night" when he hit seventy-five or so? Indeed, this issue hangs over *Songs of Experience* since the authors range in age from sixty-something to ninety-five. That's quite a range and I would think that one's experience of old age would be quite a bit different at seventy (or even eighty) than at, say, ninety.

One of the most moving reflections on old age in *Songs of Experience* is that of Florida Scott-Maxwell. Born in 1883, she was, successively, an actress, a wife, a playwright, an author and an active suffragette. At the age of fifty she began to study with Carl Jung and became a psychologist and in her seventies began a journal, *The Measure Of My Days,* a record of her reflections on old age. "We who are old," she wrote, "know that age is more than a disability. It is an intense and varied experience, almost beyond our capacity at times but something to be carried high. If it is a long defeat it is also a victory, meaningful for the initiates of time, if not for those who have come less far." For her, age was above all a "puzzle." Its changing faces had caught her by surprise. "My seventies were interesting," Scott-Maxwell wrote, "but my eighties are passionate. I grow more intense as I age." She carried, like so many others among the old, "a secret...that though drab outside...inside we flame with a wild life that is almost incommunicable....My dear fellow octogenarians, how are we to carry so much life, and what are we to do with it?" To Florida Scott-Maxwell a long life made her feel "nearer truth, yet," she added, "it won't go into words, so how can I convey it? I can't, and I want to. I want to tell people approaching and perhaps fearing age that it is a time of discovery."

I think that is a sentiment common to anyone who tries to communicate something of the character and meaning of old age. Part of the problem is that each of us must experience old age in our own way. In Scott-Maxwell's words: "Age must be different for each....That small part that cannot be shared or shown, that part has an end of its own...."

And then her most mysterious and intriguing sentence: "The unlived life in each of us must be the future of humanity."

Elizabeth Coatsworth (who lived to be ninety-two) wrote: "Outwardly I am eighty-three years old, but inwardly I am every age, with the emotions and experience of each period.... During much of my life, I was anxious to be what someone else wanted me to be. Now I have given up that struggle. I am what I am."

Several of the women in *Songs of Experience* write in a similar vein. Even some of those who have experienced happy and fulfilling marriages express the sense of having tried to be what someone else—husband, children, the community—wanted them to be. The dispersion of children, old age, the death of a beloved husband, bringing the end "to the long indenture of marriage," may mean a curious kind of freedom to a woman, a feeling that a man, similarly bereaved, cannot experience.

I'm not quite sure about this. It may simply be that we are so infatuated with the notion of being free that all human relationships that demand anything of us are resented as impediments to that precious freedom.

One of the most interesting segments of *Songs of Experience* is an interview with Henry Miller, the author of the highly influential *Tropic of Cancer*, a writer I confess I do not especially admire. But now I like him better since he said some sensible and wise and moving things about old age. It is, to be sure, his old age and not mine; not yet in any event. Miller tells his interviewer that his aim is simplification, a kind of consolidation. He admires the sage "who doesn't need anything, eats and sleeps very little, has no vices, doesn't need amusements or even companions; he's just himself, and he's content with what he is. His world is a complete, infinite world—to him." Miller's description reminds me of an old friend, John Holmes, who died in his ninety-ninth year. He was just such a man, as bright and alert and as full of passion for life as any man of any age could be and as very few are.

Miller, at the age of eighty-one, was satisfied that he had done the "major portion" of his work. He did not wish to repeat himself (an ever-present danger when you are old). "I don't want to write a single word that isn't necessary," Miller added. He also added a cautionary word about America's infatuation with youth. "Youth has to do with spirit, not age. Men of seventy and eighty are often more youthful than the young. Theirs is the real youth....It's the youth of the mind and spirit, which is everlasting."

Miller felt that he had grown younger in spirit the older he grew in years. This is a phenomenon that has often struck me quite forcefully. I know many young men and women who seem to me so old. Instead of the exuberance and joy of youth, they appear sad and grim, burdened with the weight of the world. Edith Wharton, the great American novelist, wrote at the age of seventy-four: "I wish I knew what people mean when they say they find 'emptiness' in this wonderful adventure of living, which seems to me to pile up glories like an horizon-wide sunset as the light declines. I'm afraid I am an incorrigible life-lover & life-wanderer & adventurer."

When I see young people so glum I have the impulse to shake them gently and say something like: "Open your eyes and look around you and be grateful; every day is a blessing." I suspect that our education has something to do with the distress of many younger people in our society. It has taught them to pull things apart in order to understand them better. This practice is often referred to as "analytical" or "critical" thinking. Well and good. Critical thinking has its place but often in its rough and clumsy (and arrogant) dissection it kills the very thing it wishes to understand. Our educational system scants the unities in its obsession with particularities.

As we grow old the unities possess our souls. How can we tell this? Who cares to listen?

One of the most intriguing pieces in *Songs of Experience* is "Una Anciana" (The Old One) by Robert Coles, the Harvard Professor of Psychiatry. The Old One is Dolores Garcia; with her husband of fifty-five years, Domingo, she lives on a farm in New Mexico. We meet Dolores Garcia through the medium of an interview by a visitor (presumably Coles). The story is a simple one that unfolds in the form of a conversation, or, perhaps better, a meditation by Dolores on the meaning of her long life, her relations with her husband and children and her church and priest. What is most striking about her life is its coherence and unity. Her life and that of her husband have been defined by their relation to the earth they cultivate. In old age they simply continue to do what they have always done but at a progressively diminished pace. They do familiar chores more slowly. Several times during the day they lie down to rest, usually together, eat some of her fresh-baked bread and have a cup of coffee. Refreshed, they are "ready to go through another round of things." "Each day for me is a gift," she tells the guest. "My mother taught us to take nothing for granted." When the children complained or begged "as children do before they fall asleep...she would remind us that if we were really lucky we would have a gift presented to us in the morning: a whole new day to spend and try to do something with." All her mature life Dolores has had to contend with the desire of her family, her children especially, to buy things at the stores in town; to be "up-to-date." And she has firmly resisted. Although she bakes bread every day, she refused the new electric stove that her sons wished to buy for her. The old one had too many precious associations. It was the same with the simple furniture that her husband had made after their marriage. "That is what I like about Domingo," she says: "he plants, builds, and harvests; he tries to keep us alive and comfortable with his hands. We sit on what he has made, eat what he has grown, sleep on what he has put together....Buying— that is the sickness. I have gone to the city and watched people. They are hungry, but nothing satisfies their hunger. They come to stores like flies to flypapers—they are caught....I don't ask people to live on farms and make chairs and tables, but when I see them buying things they don't need, or even want...then I say there is a sickness."

Surrounded by objects she knows and loves, made sacred by use through time, Dolores asks herself what is a good life and answers her question. It is "a life obedient to God's rules, and a life that is your own, not someone else's. God, and God alone, owns us, and it is not right that others own us."

Through Coles's narrative we get a strong sense of the comfort that the Garcia's familiar environment affords them in the wearing away of the flesh. "The head tires easily when you are our age," she tells her guest, "and without the habits of years you can find yourself at a loss to answer the question: What next?"

There is, of course, much more, more homely wisdom, more of the richness of farm life, the cows with their unpasteurized milk, the fresh vegetables, Dolores's chickens and their precious eggs, so much better than eggs from the supermarket. We would like to know how much of all this is a real Dolores or a combination of old Chicana women Coles has known and how much is Coles's imaginative projection, but the moral is clear enough. Rural lives and rural old ages are defined by the classic tasks needed to keep even the most modest farm running. There is no retirement on such a farm. Certainly there is often hardship and suffering and pain and calamity in rural life and small town life too, but it has an order often grievously lacking in urban and suburban life. A farm is a place, secure, at least for the moment, in the cosmos.

There was a time, not so long ago, when the strict require-
ments of a farm shaped the lives of most Americans. Now
only three or four percent of Americans live on farms and
many of those farms are farms in name only. They are more
accurately what Carey McWilliams called them decades ago:
"factories in the fields."

Once there was a well-established social context for the
great majority of Americans, young and old alike. There was
not only the physical space for two or three generations of a
family in one house, as M.F.K. Fisher has pointed out. More
important, there was psychological space as well. The words
"family" and "community" were more potent than the words
"individual" and "independent."

The trouble is cities. Surely we were not made to live in
cities. Cities have been the principal agents of civilization but
cities plus industrialization have become a kind of Franken-
stein monster. Industrial society is destructive of the very idea
of community because industrial society wants interchange-
able units, a notion antithetical to community life. Technologi-
cal-industrial-urban society eats communities for breakfast and
spits out "retirees." Retirees in our society are "individuals"
who are left to their own devices when they are no longer useful to the monster, who are left to cope with what often turns
out to be the most complex and difficult period of their lives.

So, in compensation, we have innumerable tales of
courage and resourcefulness in dealing with or "triumphing
over" retirement and/or old age. I'm all for that. After all, I've
appointed myself an old age doctor but I am intermittently
troubled by the fact that we have to address "the problem" of
old age at all. It is our industrial-technological-urban society

which has created the problem. Robert Coles's reflection on the old age of the Garcias is a poignant reminder of how far we have strayed from the days when old age was simply a natural matter-of-fact-of-life rather than a topic of an endless discussion and debate, one of our industrial-urban-consumer society's growth industries.

Considering what our cities have become it is no wonder that anyone who can flee their noisome confines loses no time in doing so. But this flight simply serves to make our cities progressively more unreal and old age more and more problematical. We are each left to invent our own old age, assisted by innumerable experts.

NAMING OLD AGE

THERE SEEMS TO BE A NEW RULE: EVERY GROUP HAS A RIGHT TO decide what it wishes to be called. Black Americans have exerted that right most strikingly in this century, going from Negro to colored to black to, now, apparently, African-American. Mexican-Americans have gone from Mexican-Americans to Chicanos to Hispanics (or Latinos).

I have no quarrel with the new name-your-minority rule. Indeed I am anxious to invoke it for aging Americans. I don't know who coined the phrase "senior citizens"; certainly it wasn't me. I was never consulted at all. While it is true that in popular usage senior citizen has been shortened to "senior," as in "Are you a senior, sir?" it is still unacceptable. "Mature" has been floated as a substitute. The American Association of Retired Persons, AARP for short, calls its magazine Modern Maturity. That won't do either. It implies that no one is mature until they're retired which is obviously balderdash. It also implies that the retired are all mature which is also balder-dash. I know a number of immature "mature Americans." In fact I know some oldsters who were quite mature until they retired whereupon they became highly immature. So "mature" plainly won't do.

The difficulty in finding a word that is not contemptuous ("superannuated") or patronizing ("senior citizen"), or wildly inaccurate ("mature") is obviously considerable but that is no reason to abandon the effort. My fear is that if we oldsters don't take control of the whole issue some combination of so-called social scientists-psychologists, sociologists, anthropologists, and, most hair-raising of all, gerontologists, will impose a name of their choosing on us.

The Oxford dictionary is not especially helpful. Under "old" we find, to be sure, "one that has lived long; far advanced in years or life." But we also find "worn out, decayed, dilapidated, shabby." "Of long practice and experience...skilled" seems to be on the right track. But we are reminded of the phrase "old in vices." The British like "old chap" and "old fellow." I rather like "old...of elemental forces...Primeval." That's getting at it. When we get old we get, in a certain sense, elemental. Or should. The simpler, deeper aspects of life should enter our consciousness.

"Elders" isn't bad. "Wise" has in other societies and other days been taken to be an attribute of old age but since we have found so many ingenious ways to trivialize old age, I doubt if we can lay much claim to wisdom. "Oldsters" has something to be said for it, I suppose, but it's rather unimaginative. "Sage" has the same problem as "wise." It claims too much and is somehow incompatible with retirement. Grey Bears was derived from Black Panthers I assume and suggests a fierce force of militant old men and women. As such it has something to be said for it but it is, after all, an organization.

I'm satisfied myself with "old." At least as long as we reserve it for those men and women who have arrived at the age of sixty-five or, perhaps, seventy (my preference would be for seventy I think, all things considered). What must be resisted with every resource is the effort of younger Americans, as old age becomes all the rage, to muscle into our category. I know of one such person who, at the age of fifty-eight, began claiming to be old. He had been unhappy and dissatisfied with being young and found middle age even worse. He was so impatient to be old that he came to Santa Cruz and put up in a retirement home where the average age was seventy-five. He had to grow a beard and otherwise disguise himself as an old man. Sympathetic as I am to such cases I think we must firmly rebuff all false claimants. Old age must be reserved for those of us who are authentically old. The rest will have to wait their turn, impatient as they may be.

As for what we wish to be called, that, I suppose, had best be left up in the air, for the time being at least. Think about it, as they say. The basic point is that we're going to decide for ourselves and not let some young squirts do it for us.

JOKES ABOUT OLD AGE

WHEN I GOT OLD I DISCOVERED THAT THERE WAS A WHOLE CORPUS of rueful jokes about old age that old people entertained themselves with. Many seemed to be closely related to classic self-deprecating Jewish jokes. Students of humor (God forbid there should be such things) tell us that Jews have turned their terrible trials and tribulations into humor as a kind of protective mechanism, a way of bearing the pain inflicted by discrimination and hardship. Since the old suffer from prejudice if not active discrimination (and they often suffer from that, too) and above all from the manifold ills incident to growing old, it should not surprise us that the old have their own jokes. A good many involve golf, which seems the principal form of distraction for the aged of both sexes. Some involve sex (or the absence of it). Others involve death and the life hereafter.

Many "old" jokes involve failure of memory. Sample: Aged husband and wife sitting on the front porch. Wife: "I certainly would appreciate having a vanilla ice cream cone."

Husband: "I'll hobble right down to the drugstore and get you one, dear."

Wife: "Now remember, I want vanilla. You always get chocolate. Write it down. Vanilla."

Husband: "I can certainly remember vanilla. The store is only two blocks away."

Husband comes back with a hamburger and hands it to his wife. She looks at it disgustedly. "I knew you'd forget the mustard," she says.

Not exactly a side-splitter in other circles but I have seen old men and women crack up on hearing it.

Golf *and* memory: An old golfer whose eyesight is failing him fears he will have to give up golf. He can't see where his ball lands. Nonsense, says his friend. Just get an old partner with 20/20 vision. He can tell you where your ball lands. The golfer with poor eyesight is delighted with the suggestion. The next time his friend sees him he asks how the scheme worked. "Well, I found an old friend with excellent eyesight; he had no trouble following the flight of the ball but by the time we got up the fairway, he'd forgotten where it landed."

Golf and the hereafter: A dedicated aging golfer discusses with his minister the desirability of going to heaven. He asks his minister to communicate with Saint Peter to find out if there is golf in heaven. The minister agrees. He will let him know as soon as he has heard from Saint Peter. On Sunday the minister draws the golfer aside: "There's good news and bad news. The good news is that there is golf in heaven. The bad news is that they've got you down for a round next Wednesday."

Sex and the hereafter: When George follows his wife to heaven, he discovers that transportation there is allocated on the basis of marital fidelity. Those departed souls who were most faithful to their spouses are assigned the Mercedeses and the Cadillacs. Those more fallible are given Fords and Hondas and even more modest forms of transportation. Still weaker sisters and brothers are given bicycles. George, who was unwaveringly faithful to his marriage vows, is given a Cadillac but the next day a friend sees him sitting in the Cadillac weeping bitterly. "What's wrong, George?" the friend asks. "Your fidelity has been rewarded with top-of-the-line transportation."

"I just saw my wife go by on skates," George says, choking back sobs.

A couple in their nineties go to a lawyer and tell him they want a divorce. The grounds, incompatibility. The astonished lawyer asks, "If you're so incompatible why have you waited until now to start divorce proceedings?"

"We wanted to wait until the children died."

Another: "Do you know what they call people your age who say they have a great sex life?"

"No, what?"

"Liars."

An old man goes to a confessional. "Father, I've been married to the same woman for fifty years," he tells the priest. "I've always been a faithful and dutiful husband but last night I committed adultery with two beautiful young women. "

"When did you last go to confession?" the priest asks.

"Oh, I'm not a Catholic, Father. I'm Jewish."

"Then why are you telling me this?"

"I'm telling everyone."

Sex and memory.

An old man sees an old friend sitting on a park bench, weeping. He greets him and, somewhat embarrassed, asks him how things have been with him. "Wonderful, wonderful," the old man says through his sobs. "I inherited a fortune, I bought a beautiful apartment and married a lovely, sexy young woman."

"Then why are you weeping?" his friend asks.

"I can't remember where I live."

Old man goes to his doctor for a checkup. He tells the doctor he is marrying a eighteen-year-old girl.

Doctor: "Do you think that's wise? Such marriages can be fatal."

Old man: "If she dies, she dies."

Old man goes to his doctor for a checkup. The doctor tells him he has a serious heart condition and he mustn't do anything that excites him.

Old man: "You mean I can't have sex?"

Doctor: "Only with your wife."

Variation, allegedly a true story: Old notorious womanizer goes to his doctor for a checkup. His doctor tells him he has a serious heart condition and must take it easy.

Old womanizer: "You mean I can't chase young women anymore?

Doctor: "Only downhill."

An old couple who had been married for fifty years decided to have a second honeymoon. They went to the same town, rented the same room, ate in the same restaurant and then got ready for bed. The husband noticed that his wife took a pill 1 hour before retiring. When he inquired why she said it was to make her feel younger. The husband gulped down the rest of the pills. In the morning the wife noticed that her husband was not in the room. She went to the lobby and then out to the street where he was sitting on the curb. To her query as to what he was doing he replied: "Waiting for the school bus."

Variation: Same lead-in minus pills. When the old couple got back home someone asked the husband how their second honeymoon went. "This time I went to the bathroom and cried."

You know you're old: When you don't care where your wife goes when she goes out as long as you don't have to go with her.

When you add "God Willing" to the end of most of your statements.

When people keep saying: "You haven't changed." Or "You're really looking great!" Rendered heartily.

Although I believe I have written the definitive essay on "Old Men and Young Women" I am a bit embarrassed by the number of jokes included here dealing with that theme. While it does bear out my thesis, I feel that it is more appropriate and dignified for old men to hang out with females within their own age group and I suspect that most of them do through either choice or necessity. But it's nice to know that they still have a rich fantasy life.

In much the same spirit, my old friends Mary Holmes and Charles Embree have composed the "Old Folks Blues."

My body ain't my buddy anymore,
My body ain't my buddy anymore.
We used to be as one
And we had a lot of fun
But my body ain't my buddy anymore;
My body ain't my buddy anymore.
I wake up in the morning and I can't get out of bed
My feet won't do my bidding, neither will my head.
My body ain't my buddy anymore.
My body ain't my buddy anymore;
The ship has sailed and left me on the shore
Without a leg to stand on

Wasn't what I'd planned on
My body ain't my buddy anymore.
Yes, my body ain't my buddy anymore;
It's all behind what used to be before.
Although I'm very nearly blind
The weight that others lose, I find.
My body ain't my buddy anymore.
(Musical bridge)
I've got lesions and contusions
Adhesions and delusions,
Aches and pains and allergies galore.
I'm talking imperfections!
Atrophied affections,
My body ain't my buddy anymore.
Oh, my body ain't my buddy anymore
A fact I can no longer ignore;
Some members now and then convene
But almost all have split the scene.
My body ain't my buddy anymore.
(Second bridge)
I've got rashes and abrasions
Heartburn on occasions,
Minor bumps and bruises by the score.
Let's face it, my condition is a case of mal-attrition,
My body ain't my buddy anymore.
(Musical interlude)
(Reprise)
My body ain't my buddy anymore
But I don't mind the way I did before
I now am going steady

With a friend of Mrs. Eddy
My buddy ain't my body anymore.

Mary Holmes added another Old Folks Blues number, "I Never Have Nothing."

I never have nothin'
I always have somethin'
I never have nothin' the matter with me.
I never have nothin'
I always have somethin' the matter with me.
And it may be an ache, it may be a splinter
And may be a cold when it's not even winter.
It may be an eye or a nose or a throat;
Whatever I've got, it's got my goat.
I never got nothin'
I always got somethin' the matter with me.
When I get diseases I never get one.
It's twos and threes before I've begun.
I've fatals and chronics and all in between.
I'm so loaded with tonics I'm a pharmacist's dream.

And Embree added a final flourish:

I can't get up the stairs
I can't hear what is said;
I still have all my buttons
But they're hanging by a thread.

APHORISMS, AXIOMS AND
MAXIMS, ETC.

THE MODERN WORLD HAS LITTLE INTEREST OR PATIENCE WITH OLD truths, but regardless of the world's indifference I am going to lay some old truths on the world. They are, to be sure, my old truths but I have found them uncommonly serviceable and I pass them on to my readers for whatever they are worth.

The first and for me the most helpful (I have no notion where I found it) is: "Never regret what you have let go." Life is, in many ways, a series of choices. It is, I suspect, in our nature to not always choose wisely. We are bound to wonder if a particular choice was the right one. In some instances we may become convinced in time that a choice we made was the wrong one. If only we had chosen the other path, the road "more traveled." Or the road "less traveled." A different love, a different career. Eschew such doubts. Do not allow the smallest seed of regret to put down roots in your soul. It will bear bitter fruit.

The next aphorism is more familiar (I like it because it has to do with chicken): "Never count your chickens before they're hatched." I could illustrate this ancient axiom with numerous examples from the lives of my chickens and, of course, from my own life as well. To be brief, I think it is the case that almost everything I have dared to anticipate did not, has not, come about. But in compensation many unexpected pleasures have fallen on me during the lengthening days of my life. One of the most welcome has been letters from former students testifying that they found enduring value in a course or a friendship.

The English historian E.L. Woodward wrote: "Everything good has to be done over and over again, forever." That is to say that good sustains the world. A million small acts of redemption must be performed every day simply to prevent us from sliding into the pit of greed and selfishness. We can never really solve a problem resulting from human perversity or arrogance or indifference, and then, with the problem solved, turn to another, confident that we won't have to do that particular task again. If human society were simply a complicated mechanism, an arrangement between individuals and "interest groups" that could be "engineered," we could perhaps anticipate a utopian future. That, of course, is exactly what the Marxists were convinced we could and must do, engineer Utopia. Marxists, as the theologian Reinhold Niebuhr pointed out long ago, could not imagine that the commissars would in time become as corrupt as the capitalists. Woodward reminds us that "there is no restin' place down here." The inevitable conclusion is that the capacity to do good is, in essence, the only guarantee of a future world worth living in.

I don't know that "Don't say it," can claim the status of an axiom but I believe it is one of the most important (and difficult) admonitions known to the species. It applies directly to the relations between the sexes (what is today commonly known as "the war between the sexes") but it certainly includes the equally tender relations between parents and children. When you have something clever (and usually cutting) to say to a spouse, a child, a relative, a friend, or an enemy, *Don't say it*. Even though it may require an almost superhuman effort of the will, refrain from uttering those words. It will make you a better man or woman in the long run even if, at the moment, you feel the bile rise in your throat.

Of course there is no end of aphorisms, maxims, adages, and axioms that have proved invaluable guides to generations of our ancestors. That is why we remember them, after all. But I will close with a, to me at least, rather surprising quotation from one of the most quotable of all Americans, Ralph Waldo Emerson. Emerson wrote in his journal (I'm not sure he ever quite dared to include it in his published essays), "Great men and great nations are not braggarts and buffoons but perceivers of the terror of life and arm themselves to face it," a far better guide to our worldly existence, I suspect, than Thomas Jefferson's "pursuit of happiness."

YOUTH AND AGE

THE FACT IS THAT THE TWO MOST INTERESTING AND SIGNIFICANT ages of man and woman are youth and old age. The intervening years are, well, a kind of cipher. They are the years we surrender to the processes of reproduction and capital accumulation. (Capital accumulation to assist in the process of reproduction. They are, in the main, anxious and difficult years.)

Youth is another matter. George Bernard Shaw observed that youth was such a glorious time that it was too bad it was wasted on the young. We all know what Shaw meant. It is a marvelous time, in part because life lies ahead and the possibilities are dazzling. The hazards and pitfalls of life seem remote and unreal to the young. They feel immortal, hence their often reckless disregard of danger, their lack of even a modicum of caution. What older person can look at young people, brimming with life and hope and energy, beautiful to behold, and not tremble for them in the foreknowledge of life's trials and tribulations? Young people tend to take the world for granted. There it is. Made for them. But of the making, the extraordinary and heroic acts of their ancestors and predecessors, they have little or no notion. The sentimental old refrain went, "It takes a heap of living to make a house a home." It takes a heap of living and laboring and caring and, above all, sacrificing to make a life, to create and nurture new life. One of the sweetest sentences to a parent's ears is a daughter's (less frequently, it must be said, a son's) exclamation when contending with unruly offspring: "Mom, I don't know how you did it!" Gratitude the sweeter for being deferred.

That's one of the intriguing things about old age, it seems to me. You know the price of all good life. You have run the course, or at least the most demanding part of it. Moreover, you are not inclined the take the world for granted. You may delight in the natural world, find wonder in it as much as a child or young worshipper of nature but it is the human world that is most compelling: the unfathomably mysterious multiformity of cultures from primitive tribes to the great civilizations. The French philosopher, Henri Bergson, proposed his theory of Vitalism, the notion that the world was composed of matter and spirit and that spirit was the essential animating force that played upon matter to produce the marvelous artifacts in which our world abounds.

The word creativity is so overused today that it rather sticks in the mouth, but when you are older you are more conscious, I think, than at any earlier stage of your life of the power of that creative energy that flows through all human communities. It, not "natural selection" nor "survival of the fittest," nor any simple-minded Darwinian notion, drives the world. Thus creative energy is evident in the animal world as well as the human. My favorite example in the latter case is the bower-bird of New Guinea, an offshoot of the Bird of Paradise. One day, as I understand it, a Bird of Paradise with inferior feathers, unable to catch the attention of the female of the species hit on the notion of building a house or "bower" to attract a mate. He not only built an irresistibly appealing nest, he adorned it with bright pebbles and flowers. Nor did he stop there; he, or some equally artistic descendant, made little paint brushes by munching on twigs and fraying the ends. He dipped his brush in the juice of berries *and painted stones and shells.* Bower birds were thus the first artists, certainly the first devisers of paint brushes.

Old age is not, properly speaking, a play interval before death but a new kind of life, a second chance. Youth revisited, in a manner of speaking.

In a real sense, youth is wasted on the young, but when we are old we have the opportunity to go back and retrieve our youth so that it is not "wasted" after all but rather enriched by all that has transpired since. It appears in a different light. This is not just nostalgia or sentimentality; what is involved rather is a process of integration. Youth, or our reflections on it, becomes a crucial element in an expanded consciousness of the infinite, incommensurable power and beauty and strange variety of life so that we literally live in wonder all our days.

In any event, it seems clear to me that old age must be integrated into American life. I am not sure, I confess, how this is to be done, but I am sure that it must be done and that youth and age are natural allies in the process.

SEX AND THE OLD

HERE I AM SPEAKING SPECIFICALLY ABOUT SEXUAL INTERCOURSE between two old married people.

First of all, it should be clear enough by now that sex between old people exists. If its existence has long been known to the participants themselves, it is now known to nosy researchers, to sexologists, to the staff of the Kinsey Institute for Sex, Gender and Reproduction and numerous other inquisitors who haunt retirement homes and waylay old men and women, thrusting microphones in their faces and asking them impertinently: Do you? How often? With what results? Do your children approve?

The general public, or at least the non-old general public, is clearly ambivalent about this revelation. Since they, with any luck, will be old some day, they find the news encouraging. On the other hand, many find it somewhat offensive. It often upsets children to learn or suspect that Mom and Dad are doing something other than playing canasta, watching television or taking cruises, all of which are considered appropriate forms of behavior for old folks. The young like to think sex is their exclusive preserve. The notion of wrinkled old bodies clutched in transports of desire is unsettling. It seems out of sync with the proper order of things. Gardening for Mom, golf for Dad, with the fires of youthful ardor carefully banked.

Well, kiddies, that's not the way it is. Extensive studies and painstaking research have proved beyond reasonable question that old sex is better than new sex or young sex. It is more satisfying, longer in duration, and has a higher "success rate" in terms of reaching mutual orgasm. (The success rate, I imagine, is eighty-seven percent, as opposed to thirteen percent for those under twenty; twenty-eight percent for those under thirty; eleven percent for men and women between forty and sixty.)

In all seriousness, researchers have speculated that men and women in the age group from thirty-five to sixty are so taken up with careers, with the problems of druggy children, and with stress in the workplace, that they have little time or energy left for sex. Many in this age bracket, researchers have discovered, are so doped with tranquilizers or woozy with preprandial cocktails that they can barely make it to bed and often fall asleep in the middle of a TV show.

Oldsters, on the other hand, do not have to worry about waking the children or frightening the neighbors, most of whom are hard of hearing. They do not have to struggle out of bed in the morning to catch the commuter train. They do not have anything to prove or anything to fear. They have long ago accepted each other's crotchets and oddities, sagging waistlines and pendulous jowls. They have time in abundance, and they can make each intimacy a kind of celebration of their lives together and their love for each other. What bout of youthful or middle-aged sex, or casual, or adulterous sex, can make such a claim? How ironic that the principal beneficiaries of the sexual revolution, proclaimed by its young votaries as the solution to all the world's ills, should be old married men and women.

Since this is the age of therapy as much as anything, we oldsters have doctors and sexologists standing on the sidelines cheering us on. Sex is therapeutic, they tell us. Researchers who have been hot on the trail of old French men and women (there must be a researcher with a tape recorder hidden in half the retirement homes in Paris) have discovered that not only is old sex more enjoyable than young sex, but it's good for us old-timers.

A Doctor Zwang (that's his real name) writes that intercourse is "excellent for the muscles, joints, arteries, lungs and skin. Orgasm dilates the lungs of asthmatics and can prevent high blood pressure in post-menopausal women," (that's what I'm always telling my wife). In addition, Doctor Zwang writes, "The benefits of erotic activity on character and temperament are well known." The doctor obviously is French. Finally, sex is, in his words, an "anti-depressant."

By and large, for the young, for orgiasts and wife-swappers, and for one-nighters and recreational-sexers, the sexual revolution has been little short of disastrous. Herpes and AIDS aside, there is accumulating evidence that very few warriors of the sexual revolution have found happiness, fulfillment, self-this-or-that down that particular primrose path.

If they had behaved themselves better, or simply shown a bit of common sense, they would have had old sex to look forward to as their reward for fidelity and restraint. For some, it still may not be too late. If they shape up and mind their manners they may live to experience the joys of old sex.

The Sexual Library informs me that "a study of partnered people [wonderful phrase] aged 60 to 91 [why 91 and not 100?]" indicates that 91% "enjoyed active sex lives and

engaged in sexual activity as frequently as they did their 40s."
Poor old 40s. Or poor old liars. The same source offers an
abundance of books on the subject of old age and sex, among
them Love, Sex and Again, Venus After Forty, Love and Sex After
Sixty (to be followed, presumably, by Love and Sex After
Seventy, After Eighty, and After Ninety [up to 91]).

I recently came across a quotation on the general subject
that I like. "Sex fades and memory fades but the memory of
sex never fades."

Since "recent" surveys by Dr. Zwang and others profess to
have discovered a much higher level of sexual activity among
older Americans than might have been expected (not, of
course, to mention the old French men and women who were
the subjects of Dr. Zwang's studies), I feel honor-bound to pass
along information amassed by that prominent researcher into
American manners and morals, Ann Landers. Ms. Landers
recently printed a letter from a reader who announced that she
and her husband had not had sexual intercourse for years but
were nonetheless entirely happy in their marriage. The correspondent challenged Ms. Landers to pose the question to
other readers: Do you or don't you?

Some thirty-five thousand readers replied. When the
results were tabulated, they went something like this, as I
recall. Sixty-five percent of the couples over sixty who wrote to
Ann Landers said they had infrequent sexual intercourse or
none and yet were very happily married. Seventy-five percent
of those over seventy said likewise. A simple projection of
these figures indicates that eighty-five percent of those over
eighty, ditto; ninety-five percent of those over ninety and
roughly one hundred percent of those over one hundred.

Particularly surprising to Ms. Landers (but not to me) were the couples in their forties, fifties (and some in their thirties) who made similar declarations.

The testimony was not, to be sure, uniform. An 86-year-old male reported that he had intercourse frequently with his wife because it improved his golf game.

Moreover, it was not, as they say, a scientific sampling since it was based on those men and women who bothered to write. Who knows how many others were too busy making love to take the time to correspond.

As for the younger couples—thirties, forties and fifties— who were too tired, too busy, or otherwise preoccupied to have much time or energy left for sex, that hardly comes as a surprise. It has long been clear that the general pace of American life is not conducive to romance. The days when a wife could do the household chores, take an afternoon nap, prepare a delicious meal, array herself in a seductive gown, and await the return of her mate are long gone. Even in those halcyon days, the husband often had business on his mind more than sex. When Arnold Bennett, the English novelist, visited the United States in the early years of this century, he found the average middle-class American obsessed with business. He "loves his business," Bennett wrote. "It is not his toil but his hobby, passion, vice, monomania....His instincts are best appeased by the hourly excitements of a good scrimmaging commercial day. He needs these excitements as some natures need alcohol....Is it strange that absorbed in that wonderful, satisfying hobby, he should make love with the nonchalance of an animal?"

It seems evident that the total number of sexual encounters (especially among the young and the unmarried) have greatly increased (if we are to judge at least by the number of unwanted pregnancies, the sharp rise in venereal disease, etc.), but perhaps it is the case, as Ann Landers's admittedly random statistics suggest, that sex-in-marriage has declined.

On sexual matters, most Americans, I suspect, speak with a "forked tongue." Sexual virility has come to be considered such an essential element for men and women that it has undoubtedly led to very considerable inflation, inflation of two kinds: random rutting, carried on more for ego-satisfaction purposes than anything else, and plain lying.

There certainly is no question that sex needs to be (one is tempted to say, *must be*) put in its proper place. I find it positively hilarious to have the Founding Fathers and the First Amendment evoked in defense of pornographic video, films, art, whatever. Doubtless there are arguments to be made for such debased expressions of the human psyche but they are not to be found in the Founding Fathers.

In any event, having found reports of sexual activity among the ancients (modern ancients, that is) encouraging, I am equally pleased at the testimony of thousands (is there a silent majority here too?) of married couples of all ages that they have happy and fulfilling lives without sex (or with only a very modest amount). In the necessary deflation of sex, the testimony of Ann Landers's correspondents may be a salutary first step. It reminds us that love is superior to sex and independent of sex. That sex may enhance love but that it is in no sense a condition of love or a requirement to sustain it. Sexual prowess is not the mark of manhood or womanhood, it is just the mark of sexual prowess and in general it is more destructive than constructive. Period.

While we're on the subject, a recent poll of male college students on their attitudes toward sexual relations with fellow students of the opposite sex presents us with a set of horrendous facts. Asked to respond to questions about circumstance under which a man "had the right to have sexual intercourse with a woman without her consent," eighty percent said that a man had the right to use force if they were married or *if they intended to get married*. Sixty-one percent said force was justified if the couple had had prior sexual relations. More than half of the men polled said that a man was justified in using force if he had been led on by the woman and encouraged to think that their "petting" would result in intercourse. Or if they had been dating for some time. Some thirty percent said force was justified if a man knew that the woman had had sexual intercourse with other men, or if the man was so sexually stimulated that he couldn't restrain himself, or if the woman he was with was drunk.

More than half of the students thought that "if a woman dresses seductively and walks alone at night, she is asking to be raped."

Linda Ellerbee, reporting the results of the poll, suggested that more education was needed "in the home and in the classroom" to make clear to such misguided youths that "if she says no, it's rape." Ellerbee certainly has more faith in education than I do.

The question that presses itself on someone of my generation is how such notions of acceptable sexual behavior ever entered the immature brains of the students who replied to the questionnaire? I think I am correct in saying that such ideas were quite foreign to us. We put women on that much-maligned pedestal. I've thought of them as rather frail but definitely superior creatures to be treated with caution and deference. Our fantasies of sex usually involved relations with "loose women," prostitutes most commonly, and certain women known to be promiscuous. We were reinforced in such attitudes by "Victorian morality" and "Puritanical repression" in the area of sexual matters (actually, the Puritans were far more realistic on sexual issues than contemporary Americans). Unless I was an entirely eccentric member of my generation, it never occurred to the vast majority of us to lay an aggressive or forceful hand on one of our dates. It took a good deal of daring to venture a kiss. For some of us that was the seal of a lifelong "relationship" called marriage, i.e., "Upon thy cheek lay I this zealous kiss, As seal to this indenture of my love." (Shakespeare, *King John*)

After my third date with the woman who is now my wife, I timidly asked if I could kiss her. An affirmative reply was followed by a buss as light and fleeting as "the wind kissing the tree tops." My mild salutation had about as much relation to the standard film kiss of the present day as a bowl of cornflakes to a five-course gourmet meal. I had no idea such kisses existed leave alone have the impulse to venture one.

Such attitudes are now considered hopelessly out-of-date and I have no particular disposition to defend them but the fact is that society has replaced them with a degree of license in sexual matters that can only be equalled by the debaucheries of the late Roman Empire or the high old days of the English Restoration. The image of women presented by novels, films, popular songs, MTV, commercial TV ads, and adult films is one of creatures of wild sensuality, even more avid in their sexual appetites and responses than their masculine counterparts.

Working the other side of the street, so to speak, are the militant feminists (some of whom, confusingly, are proponents of pornography, including sado-masochism). Many of the feminists appear to your average, knock-about young male to be severely censorious. Subject to a barrage of what often at least seems like hostile criticism, the males feel both put upon and put down. However deserving of criticism the sex may be, in an age when everyone is in desperate search of "support" for their "self-esteem," male self-esteem, never very secure at best, lies in ruins.

Under such circumstances it is small wonder that violent and aggressive behavior is manifest. Most young males are hard put to know how to interpret the contradictory signals they receive from young women. If many women are, as the media depicts them, sexually ravenous (what might be called the "Fatal Attraction Syndrome"), what is a man to think when he is rebuffed at an advanced stage of love-making? Speaking of education, are young women generally instructed in the hazards of sexual play? Are they cautioned not to lead passionate young men on and then expect to escape with impunity?

Retrograde as such practices seem now, most cultures have surrounded their young women with a variety of safeguards to protect their "virtue," safeguards ranging from the execution of males who overstep established boundaries (in certain Eastern cultures), to vigilant chaperones (as in my youth), constant admonition, and strong emphasis on chastity, especially, of course, on the part of women. While society has always been more tolerant of male infringements of the sex code, it was certainly drummed into my generation of young males that extra-marital sex was both morally wrong and practically dangerous.

The current attitude appears to be that women have every right (which is doubtless true enough) to dress as seductively as they can (which is often very seductively indeed), "lead men on" as foolishly and recklessly (and cruelly) as they wish, drink as much as they like (or take any substance which reduces their capacity for good judgment and/or resistance) and still have complete immunity from sexual aggression. Perhaps in some ideal world of enlightened spirits such a standard could be maintained, but in the real world, the world that men and women have lived in together since the beginning of recorded time (and long before), sexual passion is the most powerful and dangerous passion in the world and we are fools not to acknowledge the fact and behave accordingly. Until angels walk on earth we will do well to face the ancient but still operative facts of life. The war between the sexes has clearly entered a bitter and sanguinary phase. I think it vain and, indeed, wicked to place the blame on the unappeasable sexual appetites of young males. It is, rather, our sex-saturated society that is to blame and its silly notion that sexual energies can be turned off and on like a water faucet.

THE OLD AND THE MEDICAL
ESTABLISHMENT

WHEN WE GET OLD WE ENTER INTO A NEW RELATIONSHIP WITH THE medical establishment—with hospitals, nurses, Medicare and all related and ancillary agencies and services. And it must be said that this relationship is on the whole a demoralizing one. It is not simply the fact of deteriorating physical (and often mental) capacities, it is the way in which the medical establishment responds to these human inevitabilities. First off it must be said that, as in so many other things, poor old people fare much worse with the medical establishment than the comfortably off old though both, of course, come to the same end. Heaven help the poor old who are not covered by Medicare or Medicaid. Their prospects are bleak indeed. Statistics tell us that they die at a much younger age than those of us who have medical care available to us.

The medical profession has undoubtedly helped us to live longer (it is not the responsibility of doctors to see that we live *better*) but it has at the same time treated us more and more impersonally, as though we were simply objects to be kept alive one way or another as long as possible, however vegetable-like our condition might be. In a recent Op-Ed piece in *The New York Times*, Selma Abramowitz tells the grim story of a hospital's determination to keep her desperately ill father alive as long as possible by whatever techniques were available. "For eight weeks," she writes, "my father was poked and prodded. As the organs of his body failed, doctors were called on to examine and treat that part of the body. Not one doctor looked at the whole patient. Not one had the courage or the honesty to say, this course of treatment is of no long-term benefit to the patient." Abramowitz, considering the mutual back-scratching between hospitals and nursing homes, asks whether they are motivated by a concern for life or for their accounts receivable.

I have a somewhat less grim interpretation, which is that the doctors themselves are victims of the system. That is to say, the system has separated them from any responsibility for the whole human being who is their patient. As Abramowitz notes, they are only responsible for, let us say, the kidney, or the heart. They are the victims of run-away specialization. This disastrous over-specialization is especially evident in the professions. It is seen in its most extreme form in higher education, where excessive specialization has virtually destroyed the exchange of ideas which is the essence of any genuine intellectual life.

Responsibility for the apparent callousness of the medical profession does not lie entirely with the hospitals and doctors. I fear that most Americans consciously or unconsciously attach a dollar value to everything. Unless we can put a price tag even on our emotions we have a hard time believing they have worth in and of themselves. If someone we love is near death, especially if that person is one of our parents, we are often anxious to express that love by showing a willingness to incur expense on his or her behalf whether or not that expense is clearly related to any benefit. In addition, I suspect we are somewhat awed by medical technology. We are comforted by the thought that all this marvelous-looking technology can be mustered on behalf of a person we love. This may be particularly true when we know that by far the greater part of the preposterous cost of the medical technology will be paid for by Medicare and/or an insurance carrier.

When my mother was dying, her doctor startled me by saying, "If you would like me to, I will have her admitted to the hospital. There is nothing that can be done to substantially lengthen her life but many people prefer to have their parents admitted to the hospital in their final illness." I was astonished at the notion. I considered it the greatest blessing that my mother could spend her last days in her apartment, surrounded by familiar and beloved objects and that I could prepare the meals she bravely tried to eat: simple rituals of caring that comforted me more than they nourished her. I haven't the slightest doubt that the best-equipped hospital in the world isn't a patch on home as a place to spend one's last hours.

My mother was far more resolute in dying than I was in letting her die. When she tried to tell me that she knew she was dying, I replied in such inanities as, "Oh, no, you're going to be better soon"; "You seem stronger today"; etc. These hollow assurances, I realized later, were more closely related to my sense of my own mortality than to hers. I think we need to remind ourselves that our inclination to needlessly prolong the lives of loved ones is often a form of cowardice, a symbol of our incapacity or unwillingness to face the fact of death.

At the other end of the scale from the useless prolongation of life, especially when "the system" enables us to do so, is the fate of the poor old people whose serious ailments are often not treated adequately or in a timely way because of the conscious or subconscious assumption on the part of the medical establishment that since they are old and practically dead anyway, they can be ignored. A friend who is a nurse tells me horrendous tales of such cases. "I am not talking about the truly terminally ill patients," she writes. "I am talking about people like my grandmother, who developed a tumor in her colon when she was seventy-nine years old. Because of her age nothing was done. When she reached eighty-four, having suffered a great deal from it in those years, it was a case of operate or she'd die." After the operation she lived another five pain-free years.

My nurse friend recalled another case of a ninety-three-year-old woman who was admitted to the hospital with a large tumor in the middle of her forehead. "She's had this," my friend wrote, "since the age of 79, but no doctor would do anything because of her age."

I believe the culprit in most such cases is, indeed, age. Younger people almost inevitably regard old people, of whose age they have only the sketchiest notion, as having one foot in the grave.

If you live a reasonably long time your doctor retires and leaves you to the tender mercies of some well-intentioned but relatively inexperienced young squirt. The young squirt may be a perfect marvel who graduated at the top of his class at Hopkins or Stanford or any one of a number of highly regarded medical schools, but the simple fact is that he can have little comprehension of the odd and quite incommunicable world of the old. Your old doctor had, after all, grown old with you. He knew all your crockets, the sources, real and imaginary, of your aches and pains. He had some of them himself. (One of my favorite doctors had all of my long-term ailments—trick knee, muscle hernia, tennis elbow, delicate gall bladder, hay fever, flat feet, high blood pressure, etc.) It was always enormously reassuring to find, on my periodic visits, that he was still alive and kicking. An old doctor is especially skilled in discerning what to treat and what to leave to time and nature. A young doctor is inclined to think that every disability, including old age, has a cure. He dispenses the latest drug as casually as one might give candy to a child. Your old doctor knew your temperament and disposition. He knew your wife and children. He might shrewdly discern that the palpitations that you were convinced were mortal were due to a disastrous drop in the stock market or your daughter's elopement with some untidy young man.

The young doctor walks into the consulting room in his white gown, looking like an old-time pharmacist, and sees not an old friend with familiar complaints but a wrinkled and somewhat misshapen old man. "You're Page Smith," he says a little tentatively, searching his memory. Is this the one with the enlarged spleen or the enlarged prostate or the one with the tricky kidney or the old gent with the spastic colon? He glances at the file. Enlarged spleen. "Well," he says cheerily, "how's the old spleen today."

It's not his fault. He's also a victim of the system. Indeed, he may already be looking forward to *his* retirement and golden years of golf and cruises uninterrupted by ailing old men and women. The old patient and the young doctor are simply representative figures in a society where relations between individuals and between generations have been severely strained.

The young doctor sees his old patient as a collection of dubious and progressively deteriorating organs. That's of course not quite the way you like to think of yourself but there's no denying that it bears a painful correspondence to the truth.

Since he hasn't the foggiest notion of what old age is all about, the young doctor often confuses you with his parents or grandparents inasmuch as they are the old people he knows best, and he is inclined to attribute their ills to you. If they have hearing problems, he assumes your hearing is failing. If they have digestive problems, he assigns them to you.

For someone of my generation, the decline of the West can be traced to the day that doctors stopped making house calls. I take it that a guiding principle in wholistic medicine is that the particular patient is part of his/her total environment, the most potent manifestation of which is the patient's home, a key to the patient. The patient is part of a usually complex household which offers any number of clues to the patient's physical and, equally important, mental state.

Dr. Dabney was a classic general practitioner. Since my grandmother was a formidable hypochondriac, he was a frequent visitor, patiently and tactfully pursuing imaginary ailments. And, most important of all, bringing with him a marvelous feeling of well-being so that even those of us who had no symptoms that could fairly claim his attention were cheered merely by his presence. He came like a tonic, full of jokes and whimsies. He always extended his hand to me and my brother for a handshake, slipping it away as we reached for it. His genial old face was a map on which one could trace kindness, wisdom and experience. He knew very well that good health was as much psychological as physical.

Now medicine is dispensed on an assembly-line basis. Doctors go from one patient to another, spending a few hurried moments with each. A recent study reveals that doctors spend less time with their older patients than with their younger ones. The reason given is that the older patients are inclined to talk too much. Time, after all, is money.

The system is unquestionably efficient. Doctors see many more patients in the course of a day than they could in the days of house calls, but they do not see them in their native habitat and they cannot, in consequence, have as keen a sense of where their patients are coming from. May not the rise of the clinical psychologist and the psychiatrist be a reflection of the disappearance of the old-fashioned doctor?

I have recently begun receiving textbooks from enterprising publishers, written by individuals claiming to be experts on old age and aging. They are plainly impostors since, as all of us who are old know, there are no experts on aging except those who have aged. The others may immerse themselves in arcane research, distribute questionnaires, write large tomes filled with charts and diagrams; they may even fool those poor benighted individuals who are not yet old, but they can't pull the wool over our eyes as we used to say. Old age alternates between the hilarious and the tragic. Of all the ages of man and woman it is the one most impenetrable by curious investigators. These curious investigators now constitute an identifiable group of researchers. They call themselves, would you believe it, gerontologists. The word doesn't even appear in my 1955 edition of the Oxford dictionary. The closest we come is "gerocomy: the science of the treatment of the aged." And "gerontocracy: government by old men." Gerontology. To be able to call oneself anything that ends in "ologist" is highly desirable today, so we have gerontologists, obviously a growth field.

One group of gerontologists are concerned with the physical process of aging. Kind, good souls, they are interested in extending life, a grisly notion that raises a vast number of interesting reflections. We all die at different ages and, in consequence, our experience of life and, more particularly, old age is very different. The person, for example, who dies at the age of sixty-five has a very different experience of life than one who dies at eighty-five or ninety. If the gerontologists could extend our lives so that we all died (accidents aside) at the same age, what should that age be? To extend the life spans of some and not of others would be unfair and undemocratic and one suspects that those who had their lives extended would be the rich and powerful. And it is safe to assume, I think, that the rest of us would not put up with that particular inequity for a moment.

But back to the textbooks. They are full of such fascinating information as: "Women in old age seem less unsatisfied with communication in the marriage and evaluate the relationship more positively if they have the support of friends, a good income and good housing." Really! "A particularly painful situation in old age comes with illness and gradual disintegration of a spouse." Big news!

Doubtless much of the information in such works is reasonably accurate and modestly useful but the antiseptic, academic language puts my teeth on edge. It makes old age seem hopelessly pedestrian, a problem with various recommended solutions, a problem entirely devoid of either the hilarity or tragedy of old age. For whom, one wonders, are such revelations intended? The old already know these things better than any researcher can and it is hard to imagine that the young are interested. The picture that such texts present is disheartening in the extreme. The problems of our society seem to attend all ages, though each age, to be sure, has its own variations. Old age thus becomes another set of problems.

Where there are textbooks you may be sure that there are academic courses but, dear young people, don't take them. Go and talk to your grandmother or your aunt instead. She is better than the best textbook. She has lived a life and, with a little urging, she will be glad to share it with you.

Paul Kleyman, editor of *The Aging Connection*, the publication of the American Society on Aging, has upbraided me for preferring the wisdom of grandmothers on the subject of old age to the latest findings of the gerontologists. He felt that my preference for the "average granny" was "an insult to dozens of professionals across the country...." Would I, he asked, so lightheartedly suggest replacing a convention of professional historians with grandmothers? He asked the wrong man the wrong question. My answer would, of course, be "yes." I would be delighted to replace academic historians with grandmothers. It is a reform I confess that I hadn't thought of until Mr. Kleyman suggested it, but I will certainly make it a platform in my campaign to reform academe.

Mr. Kleyman revealed that "3000 qualified...professionals and practitioners who work with the elderly around the country" were convening to exchange the latest information they have gleaned from looking at and after us. The convention includes not merely gerontologists and professors in related fields but "nurses, social workers, administrators and others."

Now I certainly have nothing against these dedicated people. I'm sure they do a vast amount of good. I may well find myself dependent on them as "care providers" some day in the not-very-distant future. But I do find the whole enterprise nonetheless mind-boggling. Mr. Kleyman was considerate enough (or rash enough) to send me a copy of the program for the convention. It is awesome in its reach. Dr. Benjamin Spock will be one of the featured guests speaking on a subject I am certainly sympathetic to: "Children and Elders."

The other featured speaker will be that expert on aging, the rather passé actor, Eddie Albert, who has recently "participated in a video for the mid-life and aging entitled 'Coming of Age: A Lifestyle Program for Healthy Aging.'"

There are, of course, as at any proper conference, numerous sessions, "media festivals," exhibits, a banquet, and "dancing," as well as side trips to the Wine Country and the Monterey Bay area, and walking tours of North Beach, Russian Hill, Chinatown, and Mt. Tamalpais.

In addition to sessions, there are special "intensives." The intensives include a session entitled "The Entrepreneurial Gerontologist: Small Business Development." Another session deals with "Marketing to Mature Adults." Nothing wrong with that, surely. Old people are certainly a market. If old age is a "growth industry," selling us things to comfort us in our affliction is, after all, the American way.

Since "race" and "gender" are buzz words now we might expect a session on them. Sure enough: "Race, Class, Gender and Aging."

There are, as we again might anticipate, numerous references to "systems." I have commented elsewhere on the new field of "family systems theory" which will, no doubt, receive attention at the conference. I seem to recall that Robert McNamara, who introduced "systems management" at Ford Motor Company, was signed up by President Lyndon Johnson to develop a "system" or "systems" to win the Vietnam War. The spectacular failure of that venture also failed to produce Ford cars as efficient as their Japanese counterparts, and left "systems theory" under somewhat of a cloud but it recently has made a strong comeback. (I note that my feed store is pushing an item called the "Improved Kitty Litter System.") We have a session, thus, on "Designing Personal Computer-Based Information Systems"; and "Case Management Systems Serving the Elderly." There is a session on "Working with the Difficult Elderly Client," (I like to think: that's me!)

For my money, there is only one session that suggests the tragedy and drama of old age. It is titled, "The Meaning of Life and the Meaning of Suffering in Old Age." I am put in mind of the exchange between those two grand old men, Thomas Jefferson and John Adams. "I have often wondered," Jefferson wrote Adams, "...for what good end the sensations of Grief could be intended. All our other passions, within proper bounds, have a useful object....I wish the pathologists then would tell us what is the use of grief in the economy...?"

Adams replied: "Grief drives Men into habits of serious Reflection, sharpens the Understanding and softens the Heart...to elevate them to a superiority over all human Events;...in short to make them Stoiks and Christians."

Grief is, of course, not limited to old age but it is a frequent and familiar accompaniment to that stage of life. Old age is, indeed, the age of reflection when all of the delights and dilemmas of life come with a new urgency. Or poignancy. It is this whole vast dimension of old age that is, inevitably I suppose, missing from the endless chatter about "cases" and "clients" and "systems management."

MONEY AND OLD AGE

As with virtually everything else in life, one's relationship to money changes dramatically when one grows old. I suspect that for my generation part of the problem is that many cultural attitudes in the United States have undergone a sea change in the last fifty or sixty years. We grew up in a world still dominated by what used to be called the Protestant Ethic. The Protestant Ethic held in its simplest form that thrift, piety, and hard work were the pathway to redemption, to rewards in the hereafter. Even Americans with little or no religion believed that thrift and hard work ensured worldly success. Putting something by: pieces of string, pennies, old rags, something for a rainy day. A penny saved was a penny earned. To pick up a penny in the morning meant a day of good luck. Thrift was a virtue and a habit. The New Englanders were the exemplars of thrift. In Boston, the partner of one of the nation's great architectural firms collected the last wisps of toilet paper from the firm's rest rooms, wound them on an empty spool, and carried them home.

Behind the habit of thrift was a perception that the world was a risky and unpredictable place. My parents' generation had grown up in an era before Social Security, or, indeed, any other kind of security; the nation had suffered through numerous devastating depressions. The worst, of course, was the

Great Depression of the 1930s, an event that left an invisible scar on the nation's collective psyche.

So there were practical as well as moral reasons for thrift. The spendthrift ethic was as yet unborn. That ethic was a by-product, in large part, of post-World War II affluence wedded to runaway consumerism. The French philosopher, René Descartes, coined the mischievous phrase "Cogito ergo sum," "I think therefore I am." The modern American version is "Expendeo ergo sum," "I spend therefore I am." I validate myself by demonstrating my ability to acquire in abundance the worldly goods that my society prizes.

So, I suspect, my particular older generation views America's dedicated consumerism with considerable uneasiness. We are skeptical of the society's capacity to sustain a boom economy forever and many of us have doubts about the federal government's role as an inexhaustible provider of ever-greater benefits.

But there is much more to our attitude toward money than residual twinges of the Protestant Ethic. There is the inexorable march of inflation that has increased the cost of everything many times over in the last half-century. For my generation, the issue is complicated by the fact that in our youth the Great Depression pushed prices to their lowest level in decades. In my first job (as a bank teller) I was paid fifteen dollars a week (the minimum wage mandated by the NRA—the National Recovery Act). In that era ice cream cones were five cents, coffee a nickel a cup. Some wiseacre declared that the country's primary need was "a good five-cent cigar." A shave and a haircut were typically two bits, a quarter. And admission to the movie theatre was usually ten cents, at least on Saturday morning.

Of course, prices rose during the war, as did wages. My first teaching job at the College of William and Mary in 1951 was at $2500 a year. Two years later I went off to UCLA as an assistant professor at $4500. We rented a house in Santa Monica and when my wife suggested that it might be a wise investment to buy a large, Spanish-style house across the street that was for sale for $25,000, I replied that not only did we not have enough money for a reasonable down payment, the house must certainly come down in price at the first sign of hard times. It sold a few years ago for "a million two."

When it became clear that the only direction that California real estate was going in the foreseeable future was up, we borrowed money for a down payment from a friend and bought a very modest home for $25,000. Four years later when we moved to Santa Cruz to help start the new campus of the university there, we sold our house for $45,000, took our $20,000 profit and bought a seven-acre estate in the Santa Cruz mountains.

From all this I draw two observations. First, when you have paid in your younger years for the modest pleasures and comforts of life literally nickels and dimes, it goes down hard to pay dollars. That doesn't apply to things that weren't around in your youth like VCRs and personal computers. It pains me infinitely more to pay $1.25 or $1.50 for an ice cream cone that will always be associated in my mind with a nickel or a dime, or fifteen dollars for a haircut (once two bits), than it does to pay three hundred dollars for a VCR. Or a thousand dollars for a video camera.

Second, there is the disconcerting fact that the march of inflation has been far from uniform. If the price of certain familiar and commonly used objects has gone up, let us say, ten times in the last forty years, other items have gone up twenty or thirty times. Take housing. Our modest Santa Monica house we bought for $25,000 in 1959 sold last year, we were told, for $800,000. That is a thirty-two-fold increase. Moreover, it is a thirty-two-fold increase in an essential item— a roof over one's head.

I don't stay awake at night fretting over $1.50 ice cream cones and $15 haircuts, but they still jolt me. Moreover, I confess I take guilty pleasure in living in circumstances that we couldn't conceivably afford if we were buying a home in Santa Cruz in 1990.

Time does change one's perspective on money as it does on so much else.

WIFE INTO MOTHER

I WONDER HOW MANY ELDERLY GENTS, MARRIED TO THE SAME OLD lady for a considerable number of years, have observed a somewhat unsettling phenomenon which, for want of a better phrase, I have termed "wife into mother." That is, more specifically, the tendency of one's wife to become more and more one's mother. Not one's real, flesh and blood mother but a kind of generalized, generic mother.

A simple explanation for this development is that a woman's mothering impulses are so strong that when her children have departed, often taking her grandchildren with them, she is left with a surplus of mothering instinct which she, perforce, directs at her husband. Needless to say, my wife's interpretation is somewhat different. She takes the line that I am growing more childish with advancing years and am in need, if not of an attendant, of someone with a firm hand and strong will, both of which, it must be said, she possesses in abundance.

The form which this transformation of wife into mother commonly takes is a disposition to dwell on the husband's shortcomings. The other day I was assisting her in making applesauce. I dropped a teaspoonful of applesauce on the kitchen floor. Heavens to Betsy (where do you suppose *that* exclamation came from?) how she did take on! You would have thought I'd drowned the cat or totalled the flagship of our fleet of dilapidated old cars! She used the occasion to make disparaging remarks about my whole sex. "If that isn't like a man, etc...."

"If you react that way to a teaspoon of spilled applesauce," which, needless to say I hastily wiped up, "how," I asked mildly, "would you react to a serious dereliction like selling indulgences or making an improper pass at what Tom Wolfe calls 'a New Cookie'"?

She forbore to answer but it seems to me that the more my wife transforms into a mother, the more my actions are identified as being "just like a man," although what else they might be like I'm sure I have no idea. What seems implicit in the observation is that if men were more like women and less like men, the world would be an infinitely better place, a view, I suspect, rather widely held by women generally. The fact is I have made some modest improvements in recent years. I make the bed, pick up my clothes more often, wash some dishes, drink less bourbon, take more showers, and in general seem to me to be a model of domestic amiability. But I get no credit.

When we go out, my wife reminds me to speak to that nice Susan Jones whose husband has just abandoned her for a young floozy. "And don't forget to thank Mary Williams for her thoughtful note. If the Dokes are there ask how her mother is. She's been very ill."

My wife prefers to drive. I'm delighted to be driven, since it spares me my wife's frequent cries of alarm and constant admonitions: "You're too close to the center line," "Too close to the curb," "Going too fast," or, occasionally, "too slow." She drives serenely and when she has to make a sudden stop, she throws out her right arm (to keep me from crashing into the dashboard, although she insists that I be buckled up) just as she did when driving our children around forty years ago.

"You're not going to wear that seedy-looking old coat to town?" she asks incredulously. "Well, I've been wearing it to town for years." "That may be but you should give more attention to your appearance." "Why?" "You have a position to uphold in the community." "What position is that?"

Or, "You need a haircut. And your nose hairs are unsightly. Sit down and let me trim them."

My wife is a superb cook and has always piled my plate with delicious viands, more than are good for me as my figure will attest. But as I grow older and rounder it seems to me she augments the already too-generous portions. I protest. She replies firmly: "It's important to keep your strength up."

When the paper comes, she hands me the sports section (and the obits) and keeps the heavy political stuff for herself. "Here's the sport section," she says with an ironic (or slightly contemptuous) tone. I've always been a sports buff but when we were younger she accepted that as a mild eccentricity. Now that we are old she looks upon it as another example of my reversion to childhood.

I take all of this in pretty good spirit. My most common rejoinder: "Whatever you say, dear." A lot worse things could happen to an old man after all. He could be ignored entirely or even evicted. He has over the years become abjectly dependent and it is perhaps the conscious or subconscious awareness of this state of dependency that makes him (me, that is) so manageable and malleable.

When the husband was a modest power in the world he could go to endlessly protracted meetings, to power lunches at ritzy restaurants; he could slip off for an hour or two with some of the gang under the guise of working late. He had, in short, numerous ways to assert his independence even if the ways were largely spurious. Now retired, he is constantly underfoot (another excellent argument against retirement); his dependence becomes patent and any shrewd wife is naturally inclined to take advantage of the situation. The process is self-reinforcing. The more the poor old husband is treated like a child, the more he is mothered, the more childish he becomes. Thus, the unappeasable mothering instinct triumphs at the end as it did at the beginning. Indeed, if we accept the Freudian system (which incidentally I don't except where it seems to support an argument of mine), the husband in most instances undoubtedly wants a substitute for his real-life mother and thus becomes a willing co-conspirator in the process.

Is there any defense? Any strategy that a husband who simply wants his familiar wife can employ? The answer is that there are a few but they are risky at best.

Brooding upon the subject of marriage it occurred to me that one of the things that lies at the heart of the problem is that while men have for the most part come to accept women as mysterious, fascinating, scary, unpredictable creatures, women have a much dimmer notion of who and what men are. Freud asked the famous (and obviously unanswerable) question: "What do women want?" It doesn't seem to me that we are any closer to answering that question (whether we are men *or* women) than we were when Freud asked it. A recent issue of *Time* magazine was devoted to the American woman (and what she wants) and it even included a section on what the American man wants. The answers were quite inconclusive.

I know this kind of talk puts feminists' teeth on edge. Almost thirty years have passed since Betty Freidan denounced the "Feminine Mystique" as a male strategy for keeping women down. There was, of course, a good deal more than a grain of truth in the notion. Certainly that portion of the mystique that implied that women were weak, dependent, if adorable, creatures was fallacious and no sensible man ever thought otherwise. But much of the rest of the mystique men have held to as long as the behavior of human beings has been recorded in song, picture or written word and, I believe it is safe to say, will continue to hold to to the end of time.

But my concern here is that women have odd and usually quite unrealistic expectations of men. In brief, they don't understand us very well. They don't accept us for what we are—large, rather simple-minded creatures who, with tact and patience, can be trained to behave in a reasonably civilized way. Typically, a woman called a mother trains her male off-spring to maturity and then, ideally, hands over the task to a woman called a wife. This, I think, is where the trouble comes with modern marriages. The wife expects a more or less finished product, a male with what Robert Bly calls his "Wild Hairy" side fully developed as well as his gentle, feminine side. Actually what she gets is this large, apprehensive, rather bewildered individual *whose training has just started.* I treasure a snapshot of my wife and me on our wedding day. She has a firm grip on my arm and a delighted, triumphant look which says, more eloquently than words, "Look what I caught!" I look frightened and distraught. I don't have the vaguest notion of how things are going to come out. I am still, like the great majority of modern husbands, quite unformed.

Out of some deep sex-instinct my wife who, in many ways, was even more unworldly than I, understood this. More important, she knew that it was a task not to be accomplished in a day or a decade, or, perhaps, a lifetime. Firmly and patiently she undertook my training.

Not a day passed, or indeed, passes, without some tactful admonishment or gentle correction. I soon understood that women have the two essential weapons that can render the most refractory male as docile and obedient as a tabby cat: Sex and Food. It would be grossly unfair to my wife to suggest that these tender inducements were ever overtly employed or even hinted at but there they were nonetheless, the more effective for not being flaunted.

My thesis then is simple enough. Far more marriages would survive and hopefully flourish if wives took husband training (HT, for short) seriously. Unfortunately, the emancipated modern wife is often so preoccupied with asserting her equality and independence (when her superiority has long since been conceded), not to mention helping to pay off the mortgage, that she has no time or patience for husband training. She expects a man of "Zeus energy," powerful, confident of his sexuality, "in touch with his feelings," "Wild" and "Hairy" but not "savage," tender but able to do lots of push-ups. And if we are to believe Robert Bly she hasn't much chance of finding such a paragon in Post-Industrial America. She had thus better take a serious look at HT. If bears and tigers, not to mention dogs, can be trained, so can husbands. It is, to be sure, a much more arduous task but the results are, by the same token, far more rewarding. A well-trained husband is usually a source of considerable satisfaction to his trainer.

GRANDMOTHERS

THE PRINCIPAL BENEFIT OF BEING A GRANDFATHER IS THAT, WITH some luck to be sure, you get to hang out with a grandmother. Grandmothers are, as they say, *something else*. They are only now coming into their own in the United States although they have long been powerful figures in other, more traditional cultures. In the nineteenth century, the Mother was the revered and exulted figure in American society. Every great man gave the credit for his success to his mother. I can hardly think of an important autobiography written prior to 1900 in which the author does not praise his mother for instilling in him the essential precepts for his life. (Outstanding women, incidentally, usually credited their father's nurturing care for *their* success.) Grandmothers were much less notable, I suspect, because in the last century few mothers lived to be grandmothers. (In addition, grown children typically moved away and took their children with them.) In this century the reverse of course is true. Women live considerably longer than men and thus more live to be grandmothers. But there are clearly other important factors involved. With motherhood under somewhat of a cloud, grandmothers have assumed a greater importance. Wives deserted by feckless husbands, bewildered husbands abandoned by restless wives seeking to "find themselves," stressed-out wives trying to balance the roles of wife, mother, and wage-earner, and even those preferring careers to motherhood—the psychic cost of all this is so considerable, it is hardly surprising that grandmothers have come to play increasingly important roles in the life of the extended family.

I am impressed by how often the heroes of our culture, primarily athletes and entertainers, relate the paramount influence of their grandmothers on their lives.

Grandmothers are comfortable shapes with soft and commodious laps. They smell good—of lavender or some other agreeable scent. They *smell* consoling. Grandfathers, by contrast, usually smell a bit rancid, of sweat and bourbon and tobacco. They have knobby joints and big flat feet.

Grandmothers above all cook delicious things—cookies and cakes and pies. Grandfathers, on the other hand, couldn't bake a cookie if their lives depended on it.

Grandmothers have gardens and even when they don't, they put things up in jars. Chutney, applesauce, marmalade, jams and jellies. In the case of the grandmother I live with, especially chutney. For days the kitchen is given over to the making of chutney and pervaded by an extensive inventory of delightful and mysterious smells.

Grandmothers are the archetypal feeders of the race.

Grandmothers are also the archivists, the memory banks, the recorders of birthdays, anniversaries, of addresses and phone numbers, social occasions and all the things that make it possible for life to go on from day to day.

Grandmothers preside over the great family festivals and celebrations—Christmas, Easter, Yom Kippur, Hanukkah. They bind us to the great occasions of life, birth most essentially, but death and, of course, weddings. They are repositories of homely wisdom and accumulated experience. They are *bountiful;* good things emanate from them. Above all, grandmothers are the civilizers of grandchildren. They enable grandchildren to extend their imaginations beyond the often claustrophobic confines of the so-called nuclear family. We all need a three-generation span to breathe; two generations are never enough. Two generations are a psychological pressure cooker. When we encompass three generations we have already made a modest entry into history.

Henry Adams, with his wicked tongue, pronounced the American male "a pathetic failure." All he wants, Adams concluded, "is love and doughnuts." That may be a little harsh but there are intimations that the American male doesn't improve with age. Grandfathers are not totally useless of course. They can take grandchildren fishing and run errands, be obedient and attentive, etc. But grandmothers are what it's all about.

It should be noted, parenthetically, that in other cultures grandfathers are powerful and respected figures with a crucial role to play. For example when I asked a Japanese friend how the Japanese could spoil and pamper children so shamelessly and still have them grow up highly disciplined, work-oriented adults, he replied with one word: "Grandfathers!"

Several years ago when one of our grandchildren was six or seven and shopping with his mother, he caught sight of his grandmother in a local supermarket. "Hi, Grandmother," he called in a riveting tone. As the other shoppers looked about, startled, he added in the same clarion accents: "That's my grandmother. She's special!"

So she is. And so are grandmothers in general. I would gladly put the world in their firm, capable and loving hands. I suppose it's hardly fair (or realistic) to expect grandmothers to rescue us from the moral and spiritual morass into which we seem to have fallen, but thank God for them in any event.

GRANDFATHERS

THERE ARE, IN MY VIEW, FOUR DISTINCTIVE CATEGORIES OF OLD AND these are not necessarily chronological. There are the "agile old" who run in marathons and do push-ups and bore everyone to extinction with accounts of their physical prowess. The agile old are the dogged resisters of age who calculate their triumphs by the resilience of their muscles. Then there are the "creaky old" among whom I count myself. Their joints are seizing up. When they have to bend down to pick something up, they look around to see if there is anything else they can do while they're down. Their creaky joints have long ago ruled out jogging or bicycling.

The "frail old" are, as the name suggests, far more limited in mobility than the agile old or the creaky old. Finally, there are the "querulous old." They are the ones who, when you ask them how they are, tell you in excruciating detail, often with special attention to their bowels. Organ recitals, my wife calls them. The querulous old have collapsed into a rudimentary state in which their complaints are, in a sense, their excuse for being and confirmation that they still exist.

My heart obviously belongs to my sisters and brothers, the creaky old. It takes us a while to get started in the morning and when we sit down it takes an effort to get up, but once we get started, once we heave our aging bulk out of the chair, we can give a pretty good account of ourselves—lumber around a tennis court, ride a horse, climb a hill, teach the young a thing or two, even cope with grandchildren which is no mean feat.

Then there are stories. Years ago I read a brilliant essay in an "outdoors" magazine on "The Care and Feeding of an Old Man," or some such title. It was written for a hypothetical grandson and it began with instructions on how to start an old man. The most reliable way was simply to say, "What was it like when you were a boy, Grandpa?" If the old man was morose, fretting about his creaky limbs or otherwise distracted, it might be necessary, the writer warned, to prime him with a couple of shots of bourbon or rye. That would almost certainly do the trick. Indeed, once he was started it was hard to stop him.

The rewarding thing about grandchildren for grandfathers is that they love repetition. While wives get testy after the umpteenth telling of the same story, grandchildren clamor for more. "Tell us, Grandpa, about the time you killed the bear with your bare hands." Moreover they want it just right: "Grandpa, you left out the part where you hit the bear in the stomach and it went 'ouff.'" Or, "Grandpa, tell us about the time you captured the enemy soldiers during the war." "Oh, you don't want to hear that old story?" "Yes, yes." (Oh, bliss.) "Well, we were on a combat patrol near the Italian town of Lucca when suddenly we saw..."

All of which brings me back to one of my most persistent obsessions—the basic insatiable need for stories, for telling and hearing them. A story, however modest, is a dramatic representation of reality. Drama reconciles us to the often difficult realities of life. The more stories, therefore, the better.

One of the disheartening things about the study of American history, an inexhaustible mine of marvelous stories, is that it is commonly taught as a series of propositions and abstractions, things to be "learned" instead of things to be delighted in. A history devoid of people (except for famous and infamous "names") is no history at all. The rejection of or indifference to old age is, at heart, a rejection of history. That's what we're full of, we old men and women, history. Better than any textbook we know how it was or perhaps how we would like to think it was.

MORE ON GRANDFATHERS

PLUTARCH'S LIVES OBSERVED: "ALL OTHER LEARNING [BESIDES history] is private, fitter for universities than cities, fuller of contemplation than experience, more commendable in the students than profitable to others. Whereas stories are fit for every place, reach all persons, serve for all time, teach the living, revive the dead...as it is better to see learning in noble men's lives than to read it in philosophers' writings." Exactly the point.

Finally, the universities, with their devotion to abstraction, to what they conceive to be scholarly "objectivity," with their unreasoning commitment to the latest notion, their continuous running after every academic novelty (sometimes referred to as "pushing back the frontiers of knowledge"), have a major responsibility for the disappearance of the notion of wisdom and for replacing the ancient mode of learning by "stories" with the modern devotion to footnotes and bibliographies.

I would not wish to suggest that the only or even the primary way in which the old can, as we say today, "relate" to the young is through "stories." Some may be boring and some repetitious. More important perhaps are shared tasks. Nothing in my lifetime has brought young and old together more notably than the peace movement. Much the same is true of other reforms: environmental protection, the battle against toxic wastes, and nuclear power plants conspicuous among them.

In my community I would be at a loss to think of any cause in which young and old have not combined forces. Such unity of action certainly points hopefully toward the future. Without access to the experience of their elders (which of course is not always translated into wisdom) young people have to reinvent the world over and over again (an exhausting and demoralizing process). Without constant contact with young people, old people become increasingly self-centered, grow old prematurely and idle away their last days on earth.

We talk of deficits, trade imbalances, the threat of drugs, the dangers of nuclear conflict, all important issues to be sure. But in the long run, the health of our nation will depend far more on restoring the unity between generations than on solving the more readily identifiable problems that beset us.

A few weeks ago, having just returned from a search for the wily trout (trout are always wily) in the wilds of Wyoming with my twenty-year-old grandson and namesake, I was moved to reflect on the so-called generation gap, or perhaps more accurately, on age and youth. A third member of our gang was an old Army buddy, Bob Irwin, and when I say "old" I mean old—eighty.

My grandson's ruling passions are surfing, cars, guns, and trout fishing, in that order. His surfing has turned him a lovely shade of brown, with golden hair and mustache. His skin is silky and he moves easily and gracefully. His appetite is prodigious and he sleeps profoundly, although he talks a bit in his sleep and sometimes cries out, doubtless at a great curling dream wave.

Being with him I was struck anew at the sheer physicality of young males. Small wonder abstractions often have little meaning for them. The physical engagement is everything. Page has a sense of humor and a certain narrative style. He is familiar with, and, as I have suggested, intensely responsive to the natural world. He draws well, although it must be said his favorite subjects are hideous creatures from outer space. He keeps himself informed of the global follies and tragedies of his species and cares about them.

If Page is ruled by his passions, Bob and I have no passions left, properly speaking (unless they be for trout fishing), but we have diversions. After a day on the river we sit contentedly (if achingly) sipping whiskey and reminiscing about lost patrols, inconclusive skirmishes and ancient battles (all of which seem to have happened yesterday or at most a few years ago, not almost half a century ago). Page, who has a disarming sweetness of disposition, is patient with our stories, many of which he has heard before.

Patrick McManus, in his classic essay, "The Theory and Practice of Old Men," identifies two common types, the Drifters and the Sleepers. The Drifters, as one might surmise, are the old men who start out to tell about the time the fox got into the hen house and wander off through the history of Western Civilization. "Where was I?" The Sleepers are less of a menace, as they are inclined to nod off. Bob and I are both Drifters. Page lets us drift and even shows a recurrent interest in my war wounds.

But what binds us most clearly together, at least in this manifestation, is trout. When we arrive at the river (in this instance the North Platte) and suit up in all the bizarre accoutrements of the standard fly fisherman, Page is first suited and first off the mark, cruising up the river in long strides.

It must be said that Bob at eighty is a physical marvel in his own right—he plays golf and tennis, skis, and, above all, fishes indefatigably. Once armored, he heads off at a gait all his own, something between a hobble and a lope that appears tireless and covers long stretches of river bank in an astonishingly short time. He always claims the most remote location in search of the ultimate fishing hole full of eighteen-inch rainbows, all waiting impatiently to rise to his fly. As he disappears from sight in the willows or around a bend, I imagine he is an old Indian warrior setting off on his last raid. Indeed, I accuse him of being more interested in walking than in fishing.

Lazy and arthritic, I seek out the nearest stretch of fishable river, content to dawdle there for hours.

When we reconvene at day's end, Bob and I are weary to the bone—sustained only by the thought of that first reviving sip of Old Crow or Old Granddad or Old Fitzgerald or old-something-or-other. I am inevitably reminded of John Hay's letter to his friend Henry Adams describing ancient duck hunters. "There are two or three old men [here] from 80 to 90," Hay wrote Adams, "…in whom every passion, lust, avarice, appetite and thirst, are all gone, and nothing is left but the inextinguishable love of killing ducks. They get up at daybreak and shoot until it is so dark they cannot see their last duck fall, and then limp into supper groaning and whimpering and nodding with sleep."

If we substitute "catching trout" for "killing ducks" we would have a reasonably accurate account of two-thirds of the Gang of Three (the principal exceptions might be the persistence of "avarice" and "thirst").

The third member of the gang is as fresh and beautiful as when we parted. We compare notes on the trout we caught and, equally important (and more extensive), those who rose and we missed and those monsters of the deep who took our flies and kept on going. Just so, he lost a hellacious big one, Bob assures us, holding up his arms in the immemorial measure of the one that got away.

When the chronicle of the big ones and the missed ones is reluctantly concluded and the caught ones are measured and cleaned (the fisherman with the biggest extant fish is diffident—just luck, he says modestly; the others nonetheless hate him passionately, if briefly), we then divest ourselves of the appurtenances to the sport—sunglasses, creels, nets, wading staffs, fishing vests (hung in turn with an astonishing variety of odds and ends), our boots, our waders, our socks and heaven only knows what else—and there we are, two old men and a youth. One at the beginning, the others somewhere near the end. Yet we manage surprisingly well, the old ones and the young one.

There are, to be sure, many ways for the old to "relate," as we say today, to the young (I hate that word; isn't "love" better?), but surely few, if any, are better than a common attention to a river full of those wily old trout.

Such reflections brought a response from an old friend, Sarah Hogan, whose husband John had died a few months earlier.

Sarah enclosed an essay written for an English class by her fifteen-year-old grandson, Doan Rottger. Doan wrote:

"I first learned about woodworking when I was six. I had just moved to America and was spending a lot of time at my grandparents' house while my mom looked for a house.

"My Grandfather was adding on a huge living room to his home in the Santa Cruz Mountains and while my Grandfather and his friends worked, I gathered up all the nails I could find on the ground (my Grandfather paid me a dime for straight nails and a nickel for bent ones). Every now and then my Grandfather would show me how to do something or other. Sometimes he would show how to hit a nail in straight while other times it would be how to lay insulation properly. At the time I thought that this was all I ever needed to know to make it through the world. I figured with this skill I could build my own house instead of having my mom look for one. This of course proved to be wrong but at the time I was only six and didn't know any better.

"All through the years of my growing up I learned new skills watching my Grandfather work in his shop. Although whenever we made projects together (wooden guns, swords, boats, planes etc.) I would always sand while my Grandfather got to use the electric saw, or I would file down a project while my Grandfather would use an electric jointer, I still learned things by just watching. Even when my Grandfather was just working on some little thing to spiff up their house I would offer to clean the shop up just to watch. Finally when my Grandfather died from lung cancer in July of 1989 he didn't have remorse about not seeing the turn of the century, or all the problems in the world he would not live to see resolved, it was those damn temporary steps he had laid on the side of the house 10 years ago that he wouldn't have time to finish that troubled him the most.

"When I went up there last month to help my grandmother clean his shop I found that all my years of watching had paid off and all the skills he had taught me through the years were not in vain. This thought was one of the happiest in my life. Yet when I went to make something I was suddenly very troubled. I had no idea what to make. You see in all my years of growing up I had always wanted something—a sword, a car or something like that. When I didn't want something my Grandfather was always making something so there was always something going on in the shop. Now I realized all I really wanted was my Grandfather back.

"I guess this is one of the lessons you learn when you are growing up. You can't have what you really want. My Grandfather gave me some of his tools but I am not sure if I am going to use them much for you see it was not really so much learning how to woodwork as it was spending time with my Grandfather that really counted."

There could hardly be more eloquent testimony to the importance of the links between generations, between the young and the old.

GUIDELINES

GUIDELINES

I HAVE A STABLE OF HORSES THAT I RIDE: RETIREMENT MUST GO; THE ten-percent discount is demeaning; too much golf and too many cruises killeth the spirit, etc. One of my favorite horses is the theme that older men and women have a tendency to become self-preoccupied (not the same thing perhaps as self-ish, but perilously close). This is in part, I believe, the result of the kind of economic and social/psychological backwater to which our society consigns us, what might be called the "be-nice-to-poor-old-people syndrome." We don't want your sympathy as much as your ear. And, hopefully, we don't want your ear to pour into it a litany of lamentations and complaints as much as we do to try to give you some slight sense of what we may have learned about the endlessly fascinating and mysterious character of human existence. But more on this another time.

A former student of mine, Penny Patton Bruce, passed on to me a few years ago some cautionary reflections that her father had run across somewhere, framed, and hung up on the wall as precepts to guide him in his later years. They seem to me eminently worthy of being passed to oldsters in general.

"Lord, thou knowest better than I know myself that I am growing older and someday will be old.

"Keep me from growing talkative and particularly from the fateful habit of thinking I must say something on every subject and every occasion.

"Release me from craving to try to straighten out everybody's affairs.

"Keep my mind free from recital of endless detail, give me wings to get to the point.

"I ask for grace enough to listen to the tales of others' pains.

"But seal my lips on my own aches and pains. They are increasing and my love of rehearsing them is becoming sweeter as the years go by.

"Teach me the glorious lesson that occasionally it is possible that I may be mistaken.

"Keep me reasonably sweet. I do not want to be a saint. Some of them are so hard to live with.

"Make me thoughtful but not moody; helpful but not bossy. With my vast store of wisdom, it seems a pity not to use it all—but you know that I want a few friends at the end."

I suspect every older person will recognize, a bit uneasily, one or more of the above tendencies in him/her self. Precept number one—"Keep me from growing talkative..."—is, I suspect, the one I need to take most to heart. As I have grown older I have developed, I fear excessively (that at least is my wife's firm conviction), what I refer to as the "anecdotal style." The anecdotal style, when fully developed, can take off from any word (or perhaps more accurately, any pronoun and usually any verb—articles like "a" and "the" generally though not always excepted). For instance: an unwary guest may note that he has just come from Stockton (or Dubuque, Iowa, or Pakistan, or Norfolk, Virginia). A master of the anecdotal style, when the guest stops to catch his breath, breaks in: "Your mention of Stockton reminds me of a story. Once when I was in Stockton...." If by some unfortunate chance the guest mentions a place that the anecdotalist has never been, he (or much more rarely she) can note that he has a friend who visited Pakistan. He can then tell an anecdote about the friend or about the friend's experiences in Pakistan. Or about the role of Pakistan in Afghanistan. How did the guest get to Santa Cruz? Flew from Chicago to San Jose. Three anecdotal openings: Chicago. "I remember once when I was in Chicago...." San Jose. A little tougher but not impossible. And then there's flying. "I remember once when my wife and I were flying from Baltimore to San Francisco and suddenly the pilot spoke to us over the intercom...."

For the seasoned anecdotalist the possible combinations and permutations are virtually inexhaustible. Especially prized are what are known among expert anecdotalists as "sequential anecdotes," that is to say, anecdotes that end with a key word leading to another anecdote. "That story really reminds me of another time...."

Plainly the older you are the more anecdotes you have (and usually the more relentless you are in relating them). Under sometimes rather severe pressure from my wife (like the threat of leaving home) I have tried to mend my anecdotal ways but so far I have always fallen off the anti-anecdote wagon after a few weeks (or sometimes a few hours). I plan to do better. With Penny's father's cautionary prayer in mind I am determined to cut down on anecdotes (and cholesterol). Once I have made a marked improvement there I will tackle number two, etc. I clearly have my work laid out for me.

BLAMING OLD AGE

OSCAR WILDE SAID THAT HE COULD RESIST EVERYTHING EXCEPT temptation. I suspect each age—youth, middle age, etc.—has temptations peculiar to it. The temptation peculiar to old age is blaming it for a host of things not necessarily connected with old age at all. It is a vice indulged in, I suspect, especially by the "new old," those men and women in, say, their sixties and early seventies who are relatively inexperienced at being old and thus somewhat more prone to public lamentation than the older old.

The most common demonstration of this vice has to do with matters of memory. Memory is a strange and indispensable attribute of living things but it is always ready to play us tricks. It can be highly selective as we all know. Different people may remember the same event in very different ways. It can apparently be trained. You can take courses to learn to remember things like names. But memory is recalcitrant. It frequently betrays us. Just when we wish to call up a name or a date our minds go blank. "It will come to me if I don't try. I know his name as well as my own. We were classmates. His sister married my cousin. Just give me a minute. I feel so foolish," etc.

Now, that happens to everyone, or almost everyone. But when it happens to us when we are old, we have an almost irrepressible impulse to say things like: "I just can't remember. I know it so well. I'm getting senile. I must have Alzheimers," etc. Now that's what I call "blaming old age." If you are a faithful follower of Old Doctor Smith's Helpful Hints on Aging, never, never, say anything like the above. I have always had a wretched memory but lately I found myself and my wife blaming old age for some lapse of memory and it occurred to me that it was both a foolish and dangerous thing to do. If we blame a memory lapse on old age, where do we stop? There are any number of things standing around waiting to be blamed on old age. God knows there are enough legitimate things like shirking some duty, avoiding some obligation, interpreting some ache or pain as a symptom of advancing years when in fact it is no more than an ordinary vicissitude of life.

When I was newly old I found myself only too ready at the onset of some unfamiliar complaint to take it as a more or less inevitable sign of the erosion of time and prepare to curtail my activities in deference to the ailment. As often as not the complaint went away in time or got worse but the point is *never concede a thing to old age until you're dead.* It (old age) is inevitably going to have the last word but what I am counseling against is aiding and abetting old age.

The situation isn't improved of course by the fact that there are always well-intentioned people around to assist you in feeling old. They say things like: "Of course, at your age, it must be difficult..." to do whatever, or reconcile yourself to whatever. Or understand whatever.

Recently it seemed to me that I was having difficulty hearing clearly. My first impulse was to assume that this was simply one more sign of the ravages of time. When I mentioned it to my doctor, he immediately concurred and explained how old people often had impaired hearing and there were various devices, etc. When, at my urging, he delved into the affected organ he removed a lump of wax the size of a golf ball and my hearing improved considerably.

I am sure my readers can think of numerous other instances. We all do it and it increasingly corresponds to reality I fear, but let us not aid in the process. The next time you are tempted to say something like "I can't remember—I must be getting senile," just imagine Old Doctor Smith standing at your side shaking his white locks reproachfully.

SNAPSHOT SHOCK

LOUIS JACQUES MANDÉ DAGUERRE IS GENERALLY GIVEN CREDIT FOR developing the first practical photographic technique in 1839. For the next sixty years or so the principal function of photography was portraiture: studio photographs, in the main, of famous and not-so-famous men and women, posing self-consciously in front of painted backdrops. There was much more going on in this enthralling new medium of course, but for the average citizen photography was a swift and inexpensive method of recording formal occasions, perhaps most typically weddings and gatherings of family clans. In this respect it was an extension of painted portraits, the province of the leisurely and well-to-do.

All this changed around 1900 when George Eastman introduced the first practical film and the No. 1 Kodak, as famous in its own way as Henry Ford's Model T. The first Kodaks contained a roll of film which, when it had been exposed, was sent to the factory to be developed. The hand-held "box" camera ushered in the era of the "snapshot," a turning point, according to me, in human history. Why so? In the words of the *Encyclopaedia Britannica:* "It...became the means by which the uninstructed amateur could record scenes from their own experience easily and faithfully."

This meant that the past became, or appeared to become, retrievable. What had happened and had formerly remained only in memory now could be recaptured in visible form, a form which was frozen in time, which could be looked at years after the events. Events, often of the most casual and transitory sort, were preserved "forever." More formal events such as weddings and anniversaries could be (and usually were) preserved in mind-numbing detail, every gesture and nuance frozen for posterity. Soon every trip to a foreign strand could be perpetuated too, in the form of slides, for the folks back home, poor wretches who were obliged to look at Emily or Bill or Joe or Sue posed in front of "that fountain." "Was that in Trieste or Paris, Bill?" "And there's the Citroen that we rented in Rome. We got forty-five miles to the gallon." Hurrah!

These thoughts occurred to me recently when I found myself *literally* knee-deep in snapshots (and some more formal photos). I had embarked quite innocently on what turned out to be an exhausting and unnerving enterprise. I had set out to find a snapshot of my wife and me on our wedding day. It was not a formal photo (we were married hastily and informally in the early years of World War II). We were posed in front of our apartment at Benning Park in Columbus, Georgia, where I as a brand-new second lieutenant was a member of the instructional staff of the Infantry School at Fort Benning.

My wife had the look of triumph and I the look of bewilderment and unease that I have already referred to as representing quite accurately the attitudes of the respective participants in such ceremonies (at least in my generation). What resulted from this photo search was a kind of nightmare, a strange dream of times past, of lost and vagrant images, fleeting visions, forgotten moments, and lost faces. Snapshots. What was especially disconcerting was the seventy-year-plus accumulation. We have seldom owned a camera. I can't recall taking more than a few rolls of film, those when the children were very young. My wife is hopelessly inept, camera-wise. Prevailed upon by a daughter to take a camera to record the enthralling details of our trip to Italy and France last spring (our third venture out of the United States in forty-eight years of marriage), my wife took mostly pictures of her thumb (which, as it turned out, gave a distinctly erotic impression.)

In other words, I had no reason to anticipate the chaos and disorder which awaited me. Drawer after drawer yielded harvests ("harvests" isn't really the right word; composts?) of snapshots. I became obsessed by the thought that I must impose some kind of order on this wilderness of images. My past rose before me querulous and insistent, demanding attention. For three days I sat in the middle of the living room floor, my old bones stiff and complaining, while I sorted the wretched but somehow irresistible snaps into piles—the various children, their weddings, other weddings, friends and relatives, my mother with me in her arms, in other arms, naked, clothed, in my baby buggy, with my nurses. Camp. School (mercifully few here), College (few here, too), the Civilian Conservation Corps, the army (quite a few; since I had a professional photographer in my company these weren't snapshots). And so on, through fifty years of marriage, of children, of all the odd, trivial, funny incidents, many forgotten or only dimly remembered, that make up life. There were a disconcerting number of duplicates. What to do with them? It's hard to throw photographs away. It's like throwing away some increment of time. I threw a lot away and my wife, who professed a complete lack of interest in the whole operation, rooted in the trash can and kept fishing out discards and giving wounded cries: "How could throw this snapshot away? This is my favorite snapshot of Ellen (or Anne or Carter or Eliot). I remember that day so vividly," etc.

I had hardly finished sifting through the great indiscriminate pile (interspersed with negatives), when she appeared and said wickedly: "Do you know that there are two more drawers of photographs in the guest room?"

At this point I came down with a malady which, for want of a better name, I have termed "snapshot shock," a serious and debilitating ailment that overtakes and undermines aged males who try to put their lives, in the form of an infinity of snapshots, in some kind of precarious and illusory order. My only consolation lies in the thought that over the years we have done our obviously inadequate best to discourage or suppress promiscuous snap-shooting. I like to think, a bit maliciously I confess, of those benighted families made up of shutterbugs and camera fiends. What of them?

COLLEGE REUNION

I GRADUATED FROM DARTMOUTH COLLEGE IN 1940 WHEN WORLD War II was already underway. Thus my *fiftieth!!!* reunion is just around the corner. But I shan't be going.

While I'm against nostalgia in general (I do not think that, taking one thing with another, things were better in America and the world back then than they are now), I do allow myself unabashed nostalgia for my alma mater in the years between 1936–1940. They were, for me, golden years, formative, unforgettable years when the intellectual and moral foundations of my adult life were laid. I came from the protected and highly provincial environment of suburban Baltimore and an academically excellent but very conventional preparatory school to an enthralling new world of ideas, of brilliant teachers and lively fellow students. The country was in the grip of the Great Depression, an unprecedented disaster which gave drama and urgency to everything we thought and did (the era was, in that respect, rather like the Vietnam War for students of the sixties and early seventies). By the end of my freshman year I had joined the mildly radical American Student Union. I recall traveling from Hanover to Washington, D.C. by bus for the union's national convention. We sang the old union song: "Just like a tree that's standing by the waters, We shall not be moved." I held hands much of the way with a pretty student from Smith College. Eleanor Roosevelt addressed the convention.

In that era we knew all our professors and, what was more important, they knew us. We were visitors in their houses. They were friends and counselors (professional counselors hadn't been invented then) and role models. I was such a lazy and indifferent student that it never occurred to me to consider a possible academic career but I drank eagerly from the font of their wisdom and generosity. If I could corner one of my favorite professors in a local coffee shop for a conversation about D.H. Lawrence or T.S. Eliot (both exciting new discoveries for me) it made my day or week. And then, of course, there was the marvelous natural setting—the river and the mountains, the Outing Club cabins, the ski slopes.

We marched and agitated. We organized rummage sales to raise money for the Spanish Loyalists and talked of joining the Abraham Lincoln Battalion to fight fascism. It was "very heaven to be alive."

So why won't I hasten back to a still-pristine Hanover to try to revive old memories and associations? To pay homage to a place and to the memory of teachers who played such a central role in my life?

Well, frankly, I am out of sorts with present-day Dartmouth. I'm sure the "Animal House" image of the college does not do justice to hundreds of bright and socially concerned students. No more does the splenic and reactionary *Dartmouth Review* (the editors of which have compared the Jewish president of Dartmouth to Hitler). The Review is funded, at least in part I understand, by right-wing ideologues with no direct connection to Dartmouth, men and women whose only interest is in advancing their cruel and archaic notions.

Many of my fellow alumni have behaved little better in my view. When American Indian (or native American) students protested the word and symbol of the Dartmouth "Indians" as patronizing and demeaning to them, the college knuckled under and abandoned the name and the symbol. It seemed to me a silly controversy, blown out of all proportion by the ethnic sensitivities of our times (after all Dartmouth started as an Indian school), but the alumni freaked out and many of them behaved as if they were demented. For months (or perhaps years) the letters columns of the *Dartmouth Alumni Magazine* were filled with fulminations. Ditto admitting women. Some alumni even support the *Dartmouth Review* and engage in a running vendetta with the college.

So I am out of sorts with Dartmouth. But more than that, I am out of sorts with reunions. I believe they help to perpetuate many of the least attractive aspects of the modern institution of higher learning (as well as presenting an unflattering picture of older Americans to younger Americans). They seem to me to be essentially a time for old men to drink too much and behave like schoolboys (or worse). The current issue of the alumni magazine reminds me that my classmate Tom Braden, then editor of the *Daily Dartmouth* and subsequently a well-known TV journalist, caused a big flap by writing a piece entitled "Alumni Circus." I don't have it on hand but as I recall it was highly critical of the standard reunion, charging that the reunioners had little knowledge of or interest in the real Dartmouth under their carousing noses.

I am aware that efforts have been made to give a bit of an intellectual spin to reunions, in large part because of such criticisms. A few lectures to inform alums on the latest developments in this or that scholarly field. I remember one ill-fated session organized to bring alumni and their husbands and wives up to date on the latest discoveries in the field of sex. The session featured a pornographic film of sexual innovations (or such was the report) designed to loosen up the alums and enhance their respective sex lives. Doubtless a worthy goal but one that was not cheerfully received by the subjects.

The fact is that it appears never to have occurred to the planners of reunions that the lives of returning graduates might have some meaning and potency. That, taken together, they are, or at least have the potential of being, a rich and varied compendium of experience, of living in America in what has perhaps been the most tumultuous century since the fall of Rome or the end of the Dark Ages.

At the beginning of the century John Jay Chapman wrote: "Our colleges perform a wonderful social service: they are boys' clubs and men's clubs. Educationally they are nearly extinct as far as the old humanities go." The present-day situation is, if anything, worse. Reunions, with their childish highjinks, point up the superficiality of much of what passes for education in the United States.

What would cheer me up no end would be a reunion designed to lift our spirits and enlarge our vision by drawing on the best of our experience at Dartmouth and subsequently: a gathering of alumni(ae), faculty and students engaged in a trilogue, each group bringing its particular perspective to bear on the problems of our world and their relation to higher education at Dartmouth (or wherever) in the last decade of the century. Now that would be a real reunion!

Having eschewed (if that's that right word) my fiftieth college reunion, I prevailed on my wife (by arguments too complicated and extensive to go into here) to go to her fiftieth reunion of Durham High School Class of 1940. High school reunions are a uniquely American ritual. In no other country in the modern world do graduates of high schools (or the equivalents) gather periodically (and ritualistically) to schmooze and get a bit tipsy.

Social historians tell us that Americans are great "associators." They love to form societies, clubs, and associations. There are Lions and Rotarians and Elks and Tigers, Optimists and Soroptomists (but no Pessimists), Kiwanians, Shriners, ad infinitum. Also professional associations beyond counting. And they all dote on conventions, reunions, conferences, gatherings of any and every kind. This is explained, again, by the atomized, fragmented character of American society. In place of classic towns and communities and neighborhoods we have professional associations. People who won't cross the street to speak to a neighbor will travel three thousand miles to mill about in a glitzy hotel lobby with individuals they hardly know or, not infrequently, with total strangers.

Our infatuation with reunions may have the same root. In any event, off we went to Durham, North Carolina (by way of Venice), my wife clearly uneasy at the prospect and loudly informing anyone who would listen that she was only going because I had insisted, a declaration which was greeted with skepticism by everyone who knew the true state of affairs in the Smith household.

Since my wife had not attended any prior reunion, she saw most of her former classmates for literally the first time in fifty years. That is assuredly a very strange experience, a Rip-Van-Winkle type experience. One necessarily searches beneath the damage of the years for familiar features and expressions. They are often hard to find. "Sarah Eppes! Is that really you? Why you look just wonderful'" "Paul Phillips, I declare!" It is as though our consciousness of the strange and unpredictable transformation that time works was compressed into a few hours. The fact that virtually everyone present was about sixty-eight years old provided an illustrated lecture, if you will, on the different effects of the passing years on different physical (and psychological?) types. Old rivals and old friends experienced the leveling of the years in vastly different ways. Some were slim and spry and looked considerably younger than their years. Time bent and cramped others. The consequence was an atmosphere heavy with the inarticulated sense of life's odd fortunes. Most difficult to comprehend was the fact that eighty-two out of some three hundred classmates had died, fifty-nine men and twenty-three women, roughly three times as many men as women.

The M. C. was H.C. Cranford, Jr., who happily had the gift of gab I associate with the Southern School of Eloquence. He was instructive and humorous by turns, reeling off statistics compiled by the Class Statistician. So many had remained in Durham, so many in North Carolina, so many in the South. The statistician had accumulated data broken down by sex. A pause. H.C.: "That rather surprises me. I would have thought it would have been alcohol." The night's best line.

We were asked to keep a minute's silence for those who had passed on and during the minute we felt our own mortality heavy upon us. In our minds, I suspect, was the inevitable question that occurs to survivors: "Why them? Why Bill or Susan? Why not me?" And the somewhat unworthy sense of satisfaction at having passed that particular line in the sands of time. No guarantee for next year, of course.

H.C. noted that some members of the class had been lost track of. John Grant had been listed as dead for five years. Then one night H.C.'s phone rang. It was John Grant. "John, where are you calling from?" H.C. said he said. Laughter.

We were all given a little booklet made up of responses to a class questionnaire. The questions were simple, natural ones: "Name of spouse, Address, Occupation, Children, Grandchildren, Hobbies and Interests, Memories." There were some surprises hidden in the responses. Virtually all members of the class had married (no surprise there). Only two were listed as divorced. Many more wives had worked than I would have anticipated. Something in the neighborhood of three-fourths. It had never occurred to me or, so far as I know, to my wife, to consider that she might work and I thought of that attitude as typical of our generation. We began to have children a year or so after our marriage and eventually had four. One or two were much more typical of the Class of 1940. And there were notably fewer grandchildren than I would have expected. Quite a few couples listed two children but only one grandchild. The largest number of grandchildren was fourteen. My wife and I with seven were in fifth place.

Golf was of course the most common hobby or interest. Bridge, church, family, and music were also prominent.

There were no black students in the Durham High School Class of 1940 and thus none at the reunion.

I suppose every high school class likes to think of itself as in some way a special one. This feeling was clearly strong among the reunioners. It was the last class but one (1941) to graduate before our entry into World War II. More memorably, 1940 was arguably Durham High's greatest year in sports. Bones McKiney was the star of a basketball team that won sixty-nine straight games during his years as a player, won the state championship and challenged for national honors. The football and track teams were also outstanding.

After World War II nothing was quite the same again. The city fell on hard financial times as the tobacco factories closed down. And soon there was the unsettling issue of integration. Like the rest of the South, Durham moved uneasily into a strange new era. But on the night of June 2, 1990, nostalgia was tangible in the Omni Hotel, where some 190 classmates and their spouses gathered to see what might be retrieved of a past that in the fading light preserved its golden glow.

As for me, I was pleased to note that my wife-of-going-on-fifty-years who had been, not just in my opinion, the prettiest girl in her high school class was the best-looking old lady fifty years later.

PLACES, SPACES, FACES AND THINGS

WHEN YOU GET OLD, FAMILIAR PLACES, SPACES, AND FACES ARE A particular comfort. And familiar things. Yet it is often just these consolations that are withdrawn from us when we are old.

A beloved place collects associations in layers of sights and sounds and scents—the way the expiring sun catches the tops of redwood trees and filters down through the madrones; the sudden harmonious song of amorous tree frogs, the crickets' chorus, and the forlorn hoot of an owl; the smell of the pasture after rain; even the odor of steaming horse manure.

And then the memories. Above all the memories, of gatherings of friends and family, the anniversaries, weddings, Christmases, Easters, and Thanksgivings. Through such sanctifying occasions the spirit of a place becomes palpable, holy.

Spaces are mostly interiors (although there may be a magic redwood cathedral, a sun-drenched deck or patio). Interior spaces become so familiar that one can find one's way about on the blackest night. The hand reaches unerringly for the doorknob, or the light switch, or the refrigerator handle with the confidence born of many nocturnal ramblings. Feet move slowly but surely on stairs and floors.

Faces. One searches them for signs of aging, reassured to note that the inevitable tracery of wrinkles still lies lightly. Sometimes we are surprised to observe that a familiar old face suddenly looks younger and brighter, more vivid, as though from a sudden pulse of life, perhaps the visit of a child or grandchild or an old friend. Or, more mundanely, a stiff shot of bourbon.

The rate at which people's faces age never ceases to fascinate me. There are friends whom I had not seen for fifty years but who were instantly recognizable. Their ages are visible in their faces but the passage of time has not substantially altered their basic physiognomy. Time has just slapped some wrinkles on. Other old friends have changed literally beyond recognition (and not, incidentally, always for the worse). It is well known that women suffer more than men from the ravages of time. When my wife went back to her high school's fiftieth reunion there was not a single woman's face that she recognized and her closest friends failed to recognize her. On the other hand, she recognized a number of the men.

Another fact about the aging process that might be noted is that some phases of age make their mark far more deeply on us than others. The physical manifestations of aging are not steady, even ones; they go, more commonly, by fits and starts. Heavy aging in the late fifties or early sixties, then a kind of steady state for a decade or so, then an accelerated crumbling. And so on, allowing for minor reversals of the process and little flare-ups of youthful vitality.

Be that all as it may, familiar and beloved old faces are a consolation in old age. As, of course, are familiar and beloved young faces.

Then there are "things," the accumulation of a lifetime, some of which are, to be sure, merely burdensome, more like unshriven sins than charming consolations. But things, finally, may be the most important elements of all. They are the objects, in the main, that we hold in our hands and that thus have a special potency for us, hallowed by continual use. They can be as modest as a stone that nestles in the hand or as rare as a jeweled pin passed down through several generations; a piece of crystal; a hand-thrown bowl whose shape gives a kind of visceral pleasure; a tool or tools (I recall especially the beautiful tools of a deceased friend, Hugh DeLacey, who was a skilled carpenter as well as a devoted servant of the public good).

My wife has a battered aluminum mixing bowl. Cookie and bread and pie dough beyond calculating have had their origin there. It has a decided presence, evokes tastes and memories that no new vessel could rival. I suspect she would sooner give me up than the bowl.

I cherish a bamboo fly-rod. To be sure, I use a lighter and stronger graphite rod nowadays but the old rod is an icon. It serves to remind me of the days when trout fishing was trout fishing rather than the frantic pursuit of a constantly diminishing stock of fish many of whom have been caught and released so often that they come to the net with the expression of weary demimondes servicing another john.

Strangely perhaps, I do not worry about our children, grandchildren, etc. when we are gone. They, I trust, will do well enough without us. Ideally, though, they may miss us and find us sometimes in their dreams and wake with a sense of loss and disappointment, as we do with our parents, they will also be released from being our children to being our successors. So they will do well enough. But what about our poor motherless things, orphans too numerous to be absorbed by our progeny. They will have to go off onto the world seeking new owners, or in the case of battered old kitchen utensils, consignment to a public dump or a dusty second-hand store in some tenderloin district. And yet, for us they were art and magic. In my impressionable youth (hardly to be distinguished from my impressionable old age), I loved the romantic (and short-lived) poet Rupert Brooke who, always with the presentiment of death, wrote a grandiloquent poem entitled "The Great Lover," which began:

I have been so great a lover: filled my days
So proudly with the splendour of Love's praise,
The pain, the calm, and the astonishment,
Desire illimitable, and still content...

Brooke went on to enumerate the things that he had loved: "White plates and cups, clean-gleaming, / Ringed with blue lines...the cool kindliness of sheets, that soon / Smooth away trouble; and the rough male kiss / of blankets, grainy wood...And washen stones, gay for an hour; the cold / Gravenness of iron...."

And ending:

All these have been my loves. And these shall pass....
Nor all my passion, all my prayers have power
To hold them with me through the gates of Death..."

Like places and spaces and faces, things are often torn from us by the circumstances of old age long before death and we are often left without our comforters at the time when we need them most. Do we sufficiently attend to this sobering fact? Of course not. This is not our way of thinking in this enlightened age. Kind souls hustle us off to Twilight Manors or Sunset Estates where we get "professional care" but who cares for professional care when the soul languishes and the fires die?

STRANGE ACCUMULATIONS

ONE OF THE CONSEQUENCES OF GROWING OLD IS THE RESULTANT accumulation of the curious detritus of the years. I never pass by a shop displaying a sign that says "Collectibles" without a shudder. I know only too much about collectibles and their poor relation, accumulations. Collectibles are objects purposefully (if often foolishly) acquired. Accumulations are quite another matter. They are the objects inadvertently acquired, the odd by-products of day-to-day living. They are not items collected but simply items not thrown away, in large part because they may have some possible future utility. Or because they have some modest charm that makes one reluctant to dispose of them.

In my experience, bedside stands are the principal repositories of strange accumulations. One of my most vivid childhood memories is of being with a friend when he sifted through the contents of his father's bedside stand (his father had died in a car crash). In an instant the mysteriousness of an individual human life was revealed to me. The miscellaneous objects were unbearably poignant even to my childish eyes.

I've just made a partial inventory of *my* bedside stand. It contains two pairs of old scissors, a pair of nail clippers, a Swiss Army knife, Tears Plus, an obsolete savings book, two trout flies of unidentifiable pattern, a can of medicated spray for hives, three gold watches, glasses frames without lenses, a compass (I suppose in the event I get lost in bed), a small wrench, three rubber bands, four matches, one broken mechanical pencil and two lead pencils, a virtually empty tube of hydrocortisone cream (for itching; for what ancient itch I have long forgotten), one shoe lace, eight dollars in Canadian money, three loose Tylenols, three blue leg bands for chickens, Red Wing Boot Oil, a Jesse Jackson '84 campaign button, Herbal Ed's Salve, a high school medal for excellence in debate, a tenth Mountain Division shoulder patch, a miniature edition of John Keats's poetry, a piece of chalk, and three keys with no clue as to the locks they might fit (I find it especially hard to throw away unidentifiable keys).

Another repository of strange accumulations is, of course, the family medicine cabinet. Even if one has been relatively healthy the accumulation of various medications over a long life can be considerable, i.e. three or four medications a year x going-on-fifty years = 150 plus. One hesitates to throw pills away. They're usually expensive and if a few are left in a vial there is a temptation to keep it against some future need. Together they constitute a record of the frailties of the flesh. The trouble is that after a few years it becomes difficult to associate a particular drug with a particular ailment. Was that for the sting or the flu? For a mysterious attack of the hives or a postoperative painkiller? There are, of course, clues, the principal ones being the doctors' names and the dates: "Dr. P. Jones 3/1/81. Apply topically for puritis." What does "topically" mean, I wonder? And "puritis"? Did I ever have puritis? If so it slipped by virtually unnoticed. "Dr. L. Williams 7/5/76.

Every four hours for pain." What ancient, unremembered pain was that?

There are other accumulations—drawers filled with swatches of material, flannel underwear from days in a colder clime, buttons and string and recycled wrapping paper, too beautiful to throw away, too wrinkled to use again. And closets. My goodness, closets. In mine: a tattered army field jacket, an overcoat my mother bought me to wear at college in the North, sports jackets from my days in graduate school at Cambridge, an embroidered Mexican shirt from the days when I was trying (vainly) to relate to my counter-cultural students, half-a-dozen pairs of trousers sadly too small in the waist—will I ever shrink?

And shoes. Three pairs of Gary Cooper's bought subrosa at a kind of underground rummage sale. Who could throw Gary Cooper's shoes away? Or his trenchcoat?

Garages, attics, and barns are notorious accumulators. Camping equipment covered with dust, housing mice and silverfish. Will we ever go camping again?

Yet the shards are hard to throw away. They are materialized memories, summoning up old sights and scents—the smell of frying trout and sun-warmed heather in the high Sierra, sudden storms and nights when one lay awake watching the starstrewn canopy above while a stray coyote howled in the distance and the Kern River murmured by. I recall, was it John Masefield's lines? "I cannot roam your cornlands or your hilllands or your valleys ever again. Only stay still while the mind remembers the beauty of fire from the beauty of embers."

Broken tools, axe blades that wait to be rehung, a hoe that requires a new handle, an old saddle gnawed by rats, more bits and bridles than will ever be used, each one recalling a particular horse. To discard long-dead Smokey's bridle would be like casting away memories of hours spent on her back on local trails.

My wife has her own peculiar categories of accumulations. Prominent among them are busted old chairs. Twenty-five years ago, while she was off somewhere, I cleaned out the garage and threw away thirteen dilapidated chairs that no one could sit on. When she returned she was fit to be tied. After noting that I had never cleaned out the garage before, she made extensive remarks about my character and my ancestry. Indeed, she still alludes frequently to the episode.

My wife and I are both partial to baskets and boxes (I suppose, technically, they come under the heading of "collectibles"). The consequence is that we have far more of both than we have things to put in them or to carry in them. From where I am sitting I can count twenty-four baskets and eighteen boxes. And that is just the beginning.

The craft movement which began some twenty-five years ago has, of course, exacerbated the accumulation problem. How many ceramic pots by how many talented local craftspersons can one moderate-sized house contain? Two pots a year times twenty-five years is fifty pots for a starter.

All this is not mentioning banks of filing cabinets filled with deposits of paper and desk drawers full of photographs. Talk about faded memories. One of the strangest by-products of the modern age is the unnumbered billions of photographs recording in mind-numbing detail every facet of our everyday lives. To them must now be added ubiquitous video and audio tapes until every home becomes an archive. Thus, while our inner lives seem to become daily more problematical, our outer lives are more and more comprehensively recorded. One wonders for whose eventual edification?

I have no solution to offer to the problems of our strange accumulations. Our poor children will have to cope with them as best they can. Meanwhile we keep on accumulating.

NOSTALGIA

SINCE I AM CONSTANTLY INVEIGHING AGAINST NOSTALGIA WHILE AT the same time often indulging in it quite shamelessly, I should reconcile this apparent contradiction, especially since nostalgia is one of the principal consolations of old age.

To my mind, there are two forms of nostalgia, one legitimate, one illegitimate. Any form of nostalgia that takes as its basic proposition: "Things were much better back then," is illegitimate. This might be called "golden age" nostalgia. The glorification of the past encourages living in the past.

Golden age nostalgia often includes regret of past decisions and roads not taken. When I was quite young, I read somewhere an admonition which has remained with me throughout my life: "Never regret what you have let go." It is one thing to regret actions that hurt another; to regret them and try to make amends, or to resolve not to do so again. But it is quite another to torment yourself with regrets about a career decision, the choice of a mate, or a missed business opportunity.

One form of "golden age" nostalgia to be avoided is the nostalgia that denigrates our present culture and those who feel strongly attached to it. Examples: "When I was young, we were grateful for whatever we had. I had to walk five miles to school and I thought I was lucky to get an education at all."

Having said all that, I intend to indulge myself in some unabashed nostalgia. Legitimate nostalgia is irrepresssible and quite harmless if not carried too far, and may even bring pleasure to others.

Several days ago, when I was feeding the chickens, my shoes turned up a marble, a small green "glassy." A flood of memories and associations poured over me. I stood transfixed, my feed bucket forgotten in my hand while the chickens stared quizzically at me and clamored for their food. I saw the school yard, my playmates crouched around the ring drawn in the dirt, the marbles in the center. All those lovely colors, the sizes, the types—aggies, moonies, steelies, the boulders, the cat's eyes, and the lower-grade dobies, or clayeys. The cries: "No hunching," "Knucks down," "Cunny thumb," (wasn't that using the first joint of the thumb to project the marble?). There are many different games of marbles, but the one I remember best involved a technique akin to pool. Marbles were massed in the center of a circle and the players, or shooters, took turns trying to knock the "mibs" out of the circle. The shooter could keep all tosses he knocked out.

Possession was the name of the game. The best players had as evidence of their superior skill their impressive sacks of marbles. Marbles were traded and sold. Moonies, as I recall, would display tiny interior moons from contact with other marbles.

The pure nostalgia summoned up by the vagrant marble in the chicken yard seems to me a thoroughly legitimate form of that very common human emotion.

Pure nostalgia has no truck with golden age nostalgia or putting down nostalgia. It simply seeks to recover the essence of an earlier experience with as much fidelity to the facts as possible. Sadness is certainly an element. Lost youth, dear old images and associations, a poignant feeling sometimes almost too much to bear. Memory is a deceitful agent. It often refashions past events to suit present needs. It may cast a warm glow over things and episodes far more ambivalent and complex than we care to remember.

Packaging nostalgia is currently a big business. Millions are made selling objects whose only claim on our attention is their power to bring back the past. Usually such items are neither useful nor beautiful. Their only claim on our attention or our dollars lies in their power to evoke a lost era.

Last night, at a restaurant attached to a gift shop, I saw a basket filled with small sacks of marbles. In the aftermath of my barnyard marble, I found them irresistible. It was as though they had been placed there to catch my eye. I bought a sack, ostensibly for one of my grandchildren, but I came home, spread them out on the rug in my study, and began playing marbles. I was an indifferent marble player. The principal attraction was aesthetic. I suspect that some of my prize aggies, if not still in use, are giving pleasure to their owners as they did to me simply by their beauty.

I have the impression that marbles are not what they were in my youth, that marbles do not figure largely in the lives of schoolboys (did girls play marbles, too?). If they don't, today's youth are missing one of life's simplest and most engaging pleasures. I like to think that in dusty school yards in Iowa and Kansas, urchins still crouch around crudely traced circles and the cries of "No hunching!" "Knucks down!" still echo in the air. Pure nostalgia!

CHARACTER

I WOULD LIKE TO ADDRESS THE QUESTION OF WHETHER WE ARE losing our character. Character is not a word one hears much these days but it was a constant refrain in my youth. Character was composed of a number of what were then considered desirable traits. They were presumed to be innate but parents (and grandparents and aunts and uncles) devoted a good deal of attention to helping develop character in the young. Industriousness was usually considered a highly desirable if not essential element of character. Responsibility was another. Prompt payment of one's debts, trustworthiness (one's word being as good as one's bond), good moral character (not engaging in fornication, or at least not getting caught at it and if there were lapses not boasting or talking about them). Being chivalrous toward and protective of the weaker sex was one of the most important tests of character. To this day, a woman entering a room propels me to my feet, ancient joints notwithstanding.

There were bad characters, individuals notably lacking in the desired qualities. Boy Scouts were exemplars of good character, or at least they strove to be. Then there were those individuals who were lacking in character. They were not bad characters. Rather they were weak characters or they had no real character. If male, the chances were they would become dissolute drunkards and failures in the hard race of life. If female it was assumed they would become "loose," the kind of women who went out without hat and gloves or, worst of all, smoked on the street. As a rather moody and preoccupied young male without any apparent ambition, except perhaps to be left alone, I fell into the "weak character" category. My grandmother, who lived in the unhappy memory of a brilliant but alcoholic father, was a teetotaler, a member of the WCTU. She warned me that as one of little or weak character I was the kind of person who, if I ever took a drink, would inevitably "end up in the gutter." So convincing was she that it was years before I dared take a sip of the stuff. I was early aware that my lack of character was a general topic of conversation in the extended family. Various remedies were proposed and debated. And some were tried. Military school was tried without any signs of a strengthened character (I got a terrible case of poison oak).

Somehow I managed to muddle along without much character. I remember my mother, who always looked on the bright side of things and loved me dearly despite my lack of character, once replied to my grandfather's familiar inventory of my shortcomings by saying cheerily, "Well, Father, you have to admit that there's nothing mean about Page." I'm not sure this was true in fact, but my grandfather generously concurred. Meanness (or the lack of it) was not in any event a strong plus or minus character-wise.

In any event, it turned out that my lack of character was not fatal due in large part to the fact that I was smart enough (or lucky enough) to marry a woman who had more than enough character for the two of us (not to mention our children and grandchildren). Needless to say, I got no credit, at least initially, for marrying a woman of character. The fact that without a job, or any career plan, or any income other than the modest, temporary pay of a second lieutenant in the Army of the United States, I would ask a poor, impressionable young Southern woman to marry me and, when she consented, go ahead and marry her in face of the outspoken opposition of my family and hers appeared to ratify all the misgivings about my character.

In any event, the notion of character appears to have become as extinct as the dodo. I haven't heard anyone use the word in decades. I constantly encounter people, young and old, who have very little character of any kind. To be sure bad characters abound, but they are viewed in the main as helpless victims of society unless, of course, they happen to be home-less in which case they are denounced as deadbeats and bums.

I confess to a lingering fondness for the whole notion of character—good, bad, weak. Whatever. It was a valuable mea-suring stick, a constant reminder of the hard realities of the world outside. It's not too much, I think, to say that charac-ter—honesty, responsibility, old-fashioned morality, and a vast amount of very hard work, made the United States what it is today, for better or worse, largely for the better.

ODD APPETITES

Every nation/society/culture has its own unique relationship to food. The United States is, in this respect, no different from Thailand or Japan or Mexico. Americans are perhaps most notable for the quantity of food consumed and the speed with which we consume it. And our obsession with trying to mitigate the consequence of our eating habits, i.e. losing weight. Foreign visitors have, since the early years of the republic, been astonished at the abundance of food, its low cost, and the prodigious amounts put away by individual eaters. Many immigrants came to America from countries where the poor often went hungry and sometimes, as in the terrible Irish potato famine, starved to death. So, it seems safe to assume, eating has a kind of psychological significance for many Americans. It has been a way of asserting or confirming a victory over hunger and want. In the 1820s, an itinerant Swiss Bible salesman, Johannes Schweitzer, coming on "the poor hut of a daily laborer" at meal time was invited to stay for dinner. Instead of "the meager meal," Schweitzer expected, "there were," he noted with astonishment, "sausages, ham, a guinea hen, cabbage and salad, butter, white bread, jam, and an apple pie on the table."

The supermarket, a classic American invention, is perhaps the most revealing symbol of our collective psyche. And of our own relation to food. It is, in the words of my friend Charles Embree's "Supermarket Song," a place where "everything outside is inside." I suspect that if we allowed the implications of the supermarket to sink in when we went shopping we would faint dead away.

But my topic is, more specifically, the relationship of food to old age. Just as old age brings with it, almost invariably, "strange accumulations," it brings "odd appetites." If my own experience is in any way representative, old age is, in respect to sudden hungers for odd food items, rather like pregnancy. Whether there is a physiological basis for such appetites I cannot say, but there are obvious psychological ones. Taste (closely followed by sound) is the sense that is most apt to unlock memory. Marcel Proust made the taste of a petit madeleine the key that unlocked the *Rembrance of Things Past*, the title of his great novel. I suppose we have what might be called a "taste memory," an unexplored circuitry that triggers long-forgotten associations. Does the lonesome cry of a distant train stimulate a hunger for Sugar Babies from a childhood penny-candy store? Or a scratchy record of "Yes, We Have No Bananas?" make us yearn for a chocolate sundae?

Such unbidden appetites are usually as transitory as they are unexpected. I have gone through a jelly bean phase and a vanilla milk shake phase and even, most disconcerting of all, a candy corn phase. Also a rock candy phase and a horehound candy phase.

But there is more to food and old age than odd and unexpected appetites. There is the practical, material, regular, everyday, run-of-the-mill food not associated with any particular memory: here we observe a fierce concentration on food.

I recall as a child seeing old men and women bent over chocolate sodas at the local ice cream parlor with an intense absorption that puzzled me. I see the same kind of absorption among my contemporaries today. It sometimes seems as though the food itself, or at least its quality, is less important to old eaters than what I suppose might be called the *process of eating*, the chewing and swallowing. Can it be that eating is here a kind of affirmation of life itself? As life inevitably constricts, does food become more and more important, an assertion of vitality, a sacrament? I have told the story of the two old philosophers and friends, Voltaire and Fénelon, who were dining together when Fénelon fell over dead. As the story goes, Voltaire called out to the footman, "I'll have his dessert." I told the tale as an example of the self-centeredness that often characterizes old age. It perhaps serves equally well as an illustration of the importance that food assumes as we grow old.

So there are really two issues involving old folks and food. First, there are these odd appetites that possess us, that come and go like vagrant memories. These are, I suspect, more comic than calamitous. As to the other, the fixation on food, I am not so sure. Here, I suspect, we had best be on guard. "Enjoy," as they say. But not too much lest we lose our souls.

Sleep and Dreams

Since we spend approximately one-third of our lives sleeping (or trying to sleep) it is not surprising that the nature of sleep should be a major concern of the species and the subject of poets, philosophers, theologians and, more recently, psychologists. Surely the most memorable lines on sleep, as on so many others aspects of life, are Shakespeare's:

Sleep that knits up the ravell'd sleeve of care,
The death of each day's life, sore labor's bath,
Balm of hurt minds, great nature's second course,
Chief nourisher of life's feasts.

Although the Psalmist assures us that sleep is one of the Lord's most precious gifts ("He giveth his beloved sleep"), the fact is that Americans are notoriously poor sleepers. In colonial America one school of sleep researchers was convinced that night air was little short of lethal, full of "noxious vapors" and dangerous "miasmas." Good health required that the sleeper allow no vagrant breeze in his or her bedchamber. A rival school, of which, incidentally, Benjamin Franklin was the most conspicuous spokesman, insisted that fresh air was essential to rejuvenating slumber.

The advocates of fresh air gained ground with each decade. In 1861 Dr. W.W. Hall published a book called, bluntly enough, *Sleep*. His thesis was a simple one. "It is the aim and end of this Book," he wrote, "to show that as a means of high health, good blood, and a strong mind to old and young, one sick or well, each should have a single bed in a large, clean, light room, so as to pass hours of sleep in a pure, fresh air...." The alternative, the doctor warned, was premature death.

When *The Witchery of Sleep* appeared in 1903, it covered such practical matters as "night apparel," bed design, the composition of mattresses and bedclothes but it had more to say about sleep's "poetical, refining beauty and its marvelous import to human life." "Pure, fresh air" became, in fact, a fad and an obsession. One result was the sleeping porch era. Every progressive, middle-class home must have a sleeping porch to which the children of the family were consigned in fair weather and foul.

But fresh air, salubrious as it might be, could not cure the nation's principal cause of sleeplessness—the hectic pace of American life, augmented by too much coffee and indigestible food. (Recognition of the relationship between proper diet and restful sleep is at least as old as the Old Testament; the author of Ecclesiastes reminds us, "Sound sleep comes of moderate eating.") As to the hectic pace of American urban life in the 1840s, the New York lawyer, George Templeton Strong, lamented the fact that he could get through the days only by drinking innumerable cups of coffee. Then at night he had to take sleeping potions in order to be able to get a night's rest. Similarly today, the typical upwardly mobile American thinks nothing of gulping down a richly indigestible meal (often preceded by several cocktails and accompanied by wine or beer), then turning to work-brought-home or rushing off to attend an emotion-loaded meeting, or watching a horrendous docudrama full of death and violence and then toddling off to bed expecting a night of untroubled slumber. Good luck! I date my emancipation, sleep-wise, from the day my Nepalese friend and colleague, Bhuwan Joshi, told my class (on the chicken) of a prayer taught Hindu children as a kind of rite of passage, a prayer to be said each day at sundown. It went, as I recall, something like this: "Great Vishnu [or Brahma] now that day is ending and night is about to descend, help me to compose my spirit and prepare to greet the good night and the blessed sleep it brings." The prayer, or at least the idea of the prayer, made a profound impression on me. I thought ruefully of how little attention we pay to the natural rhythms of our lives, how lacking in respect we are for the diurnal cycle of the hours, how foolishly we expend our energies, and I resolved to try, so far as I could, to take to heart the theme of the prayer: quite simply, not to do things after dusk that belonged more appropriately to the hurried hours of the day, to, in short, prepare myself physically and psychologically for the gift of night and sleep. And by and large I have adhered to the spirit if not always to the letter of my friend Joshi's prayer. No sleeping potion has crossed my lips in twenty years and I sleep well enough for my age.

Which brings me to the issue of sleep and the various ages of man (and, I assume, of woman). We speak of the deep, untroubled sleep of youth. I observe it enviously in my grandchildren. Then there is the sleep of adults which, if we are to judge by the nostrums on drugstore counters and the research of the experts, is a disaster area shadowed by the anxieties and frustrations with which our society abounds.

Finally, there is the sleep of old age, quite a different matter. In old age one is acutely aware of, among other things, the relation of sleep to death. Shelley's words have a special poignancy: "How wonderful is death, and his brother sleep." Another poet calls sleep "brother of quiet death, when life is too, too, long!"

The sleep of old age is most often fitful, interrupted now and again by pressing needs. Wakings are longer, reflections deeper. Three o'clock in the morning is a typical hour of reckoning, a time when one's life spins by: thoughts of things done and undone, of loves lost and loves sustained. Then there are old aches and pains, which further inhibit slumber. Sleep, when it comes, is lighter, but, I suspect, sweeter in many ways because the days and nights have fallen into complementary patterns and dreams are often more benign that those in more stressful times.

Perhaps we should give the famous nineteenth-century eccentric, George Frances Train, the last word. He wrote: "Seventy-four years young, I am good for twice that by economizing life. You want five lines on sleep! I want eight hours!" I'll certainly settle for eight hours.

Like sleep, the dreams of the old are quite different from the dreams of the young. The dream researchers tell us that all human beings from unborn infants (what *could* they dream about?) to nonagenarians dream. The only creature that does not dream, we are told, is the anteater. Happy the anteater!

I often reflect on having lived in a century that has seen that the rise (and fall) of those twin gods of the modern age, Marx and Freud. A psychologist named Allan Hobson has pretty well made a shambles of the Freudian interpretation of dreams (it should be noted that he has by no means persuaded all psychotherapists of the truth of his iconoclastic views).

He had no trouble persuading me. I was already there, so to speak. To Freud, dreams were revelations of neurotic symptoms and were to be understood primarily as sublimated erotic fantasies. That always seemed to me a depressingly mundane view of the mysterious and inexplicable character of dreams. I have treasured George Bernard Shaw's comment that he had been fascinated by dreams until he read Freud's treatise on the subject. In any event, it seems evident that dreams or no dreams, Sigmund has had his day.

The dream researchers tell us that dreams, as indicated by REM (Rapid Eye Movement), begin some ninety minutes after we fall asleep, continue for another ninety minutes, and we then revert to a deep and more-or-less dreamless sleep. This, I must say, is not my experience. It fails to take account of naps. Haven't all of us dozed off and dreamt instantly and vividly? Whether these ninety-minute cycles of active dreaming and deep, usually dreamless sleep exist more in the imaginations of sleep researchers than in ordinary human beings is in a sense beside the point; we plainly have to dream. What remains beyond the ken of the researchers is the purpose of dreaming and, of course, whether dreams are in some way capable of interpretation. Whether, to put the matter as directly as possible, dreams are an avenue of access to our subconscious, whether they reveal some essential but otherwise hidden clue to our personalities. Since I don't believe in the subconscious and have never consciously encountered the subconscious, I am obviously skeptical about the usefulness of dreams to psychotherapists. I am also reassured as to the second point by Allan Hobson's statement that he has never discovered anything about a patient through an analysis of his or her dreams that he hadn't already discerned by talking to and observing said patient.

It seems to me that there are two or three quite different categories of dreams. There are dreams that are just what they seem to be—dreams of trying to find a bathroom (increasingly common in old age), dreams of erotic conquest (ageless), dreams of finding money or valuable and highly desired "things." Dreams of doing effortlessly what in real life is plainly difficult or impossible. I have frequent dreams of running effortlessly over forbidding terrain. The more my old joints creak, the more I dream of gliding through space. There are dreams that revolve around intractable problems, around feelings of guilt. Sometimes I have been exonerated in dreams for faults and failings. I used to dream, from time to time, that the secret of life was about to be revealed to me; unfortunately I always woke up before the revelation.

Then, of course, there are dreams that are utterly mysterious, that seem without rhyme or reason. There are nightmares, terrifying dreams, dreams of danger and imminent death. These we could all clearly do without. Sweet dreams, we say. Sweet dreams we hope for, but dreams are clearly the one aspect of our lives over which we have little or no control. Most dreams are as ephemeral as dew on the morning grass, yet some remain in memory for a lifetime.

The dream researchers have discovered childrens' dreams are very different from the dreams of adults. The dreams of the old are different from the dreams of the young and of the middle-aged as well. So far as I know, the sleep/dream researchers have paid little attention to the dreams of old age. The British philosopher, Thomas Hobbes, wrote in 1651, "Old men commonly dream oftener, and have their dreams more painful than the young." Is that true?

The most mysterious thing about dreams is *how boring accounts of other people's dreams are* to me. When I awake from a particularly fascinating or bizarre dream and try to tell my wife about it, her eyes glaze over and a look of complete detachment falls over her normally cheerful countenance. And vice versa. With the number of psychoanalysts rapidly diminishing who will listen to our dreams, who will listen to us? I fear the answer is nobody.

And then there are naps. Naps are a privilege (and a pleasure) of old age. "Naps" is certainly an odd word. The dictionary is not particularly helpful, informing us that it is derived from the Anglo-Saxon word "knappian." The dictionary equates it, misleadingly, in my opinion, with "drowsy," which is quite another matter altogether.

You don't have to be old, of course, to nap. You can be very young. "It's time for your nap, dear," is the immemorial cry of desperate mothers. I myself have been addicted to the nap since childhood, but in our culture to be caught napping has definitely discreditable connotations. Americans want to be on the ball, making money, getting ahead. No time for napping. Ever since the Cold War began we have lived in collective terror of being caught napping by the Russians who presumably stay up all night (or used to) just to catch us napping. Two thousand tanks or five hundred missiles behind. Keep awake, Americans!

There are many different kinds of naps.

Among the naps I am most fond of is the famous afternoon nap which follows a tasty lunch with a glass of wine or a bottle of beer. Perhaps a little classical music playing softly in the background. I drift off blissfully, in and out of sleep per se, and wake refreshed and ready for whatever the rest of the day may bring.

There are early morning naps. For my wife and me, they are more frequent as we get older. Often, after a restless night, we wake at dawn, exchange a few sleepy words, snuggle up and take our respective naps until the sun is well up. The morning air is soft and scented, the sunlight mild and golden. Like the afternoon nap, the early morning naps are wonderfully refreshing.

Inadvertent naps catch you by surprise while you're reading or watching television. We had to give up videos because we invariably napped before the end. "What happened?" I would ask my wife the next morning. "I have no idea. I napped just after the killer drew his gun."

Perhaps my favorite naps are the furtive ones I catch in the midst of a commencement address (one of the least rewarding of all forensic forms), or a boring lecture that I have gone to against my better judgment. I go to virtually all lectures against my better judgment, a judgment formed over fifty years of listening to lectures as infrequently as possible. The only exceptions are lectures by Mary Holmes, Norman O. Brown, and Paul Lee. The trick in napping during a lecture is to position oneself in such a manner as to appear to be listening intently. A hand over one's eyes will hopefully conceal the fact that they are closed. With indifferently played music one can feign intense concentration with closed eyes. It is important when napping during a sermon, lecture, or concert to incline forward, thus avoiding the awkwardness of having one's head fall back with mouth open, and, most humiliating of all, emitting a riveting snore. My wife, who can instantly recognize the most carefully camouflaged nap, usually gives me a firm nudge in the ribs. The result has been a certain thickness and numbness of the rib cage on my right side. (She always sits to my right. Do all wives sit to their husband's right?)

In civilized nations the nap has been institutionalized. In Mediterranean countries a two-hour lunch period allows for a proper postprandial snooze or some other form of recreational activity. In the Hispanic world it's a siesta. I am convinced Americans would all be better off if we adopted such a practice. It would do our nervous systems a world of good, not to mention our digestive systems. And relieve that wretched stress we're always yammering about.

Perhaps the most famous napper in recent American history was ex-President Ronald Reagan. The President was following in the footsteps of his hero Calvin Coolidge, another famous napper. The rather mad ebullience with which the former President greeted the world (and which Nancy now admits often got her goat) may well have been the consequence of his well-documented naps. We should all, I'm sure, be grateful about naps rather than censorious. When the President was awake he was up to all kinds of mischief—running up the deficit, promoting star wars, trading arms for hostages, devising new strategies to bash the Sandinistas. Even longer naps would have been to the benefit of the nation. So, as I say, I am in favor of naps for everyone. I suspect naps would be the surest way to produce that "kinder, gentler America" that former President Bush encouraged us to hope for.

LAUGHTER AND TEARS

WE SEEM TO HAVE AN INCLINATION TO TRY TO FIND AN APPROPRIATE name for our age, the very odd times we live in (as the Age of Anxiety, the Nuclear Age, the Cold War Era, etc.). An equally appropriate name, I suspect, would be the Therapeutic Age. Our era, or epoch, seems to abound in an extraordinary range of illness of body and soul, especially the latter. Things that we used to do for the joy of doing them are now urged on us as therapy, hence art therapy, dance therapy, music therapy, and so on ad infinitum.

Another manifestation of the therapeutic impulse is the innumerable support groups offering consolation (therapy) for every conceivable human disability, anxiety, or emotional need. This, in turn, appears to be related to what *Time* magazine referred to a few weeks back as "Crybabyism," the conviction that life has dealt you a bad hand one way or another, and someone else is to blame, and someone has to pay in dollars and cents, or, more commonly, in confessions of guilt or some form of retribution.

There are support groups for those with "substance abuse" problems with cigarettes, booze, cocaine, pot, heroin, chocolate candy, as well as other problems: too fat, too thin, too tall, too short. And then there are support groups for the friends and relatives of those with problems, the wives of alcoholics and drug addicts. The morning paper brings me news of a meeting of the local Pet Loss Support group.

Then, of course, there are support groups for every ethnic minority. These are especially in evidence on college campuses where some students report strong pressure from their fellow-ethnics "not to associate with students who are not of their ethnic background."

Perhaps I need not belabor the point. I'm sure there must be support groups yet to come to my attention whose mission it is to support those of us who are growing older than we wish to be. Like my wife who just turned seventy. A support group for seventy-year-old women, five feet three inches tall, former-ly blond now gray, who weigh a bit more than they wish and are married to older men who are not especially sympathetic to their problem.

Of course there is the cruise line business, which has fat-tened on, or is it "battened on," the old and restless. A com-muniqué from the National Tour Association announces that next to reading, "mature adults" (I love that designation) like to travel. Those who like to travel consider themselves "young and adventurous in spirit," the association's bulletin informs me. I must say I would describe them somewhat differently: perhaps "perpetually optimistic," "foolhardy dreamers," etc.

However that may be, I see no reason why travel agents should not be designated as "Age Therapists," men and women dedicated to dispatching old people around the world under circumstances that often make old age seem like a def-initely minor disability.

Which brings me to my main point. Laughter and tears. Laughter and tears, we are now told (as the result of the latest research by psychologists, sociologists, socialists, and other pathologists), are therapeutic. This line of investigation was opened a few years back by Norman Cousins who maintained that laughing a lot had enabled him to recover from a near-fatal illness in record time. As I recall, he speeded the healing process by watching old Laurel and Hardy films and laughing 'till he fell out of bed. Some "researchers" were hot on the trail of laughter as therapy. They confirmed Cousins's theory. Yes, laughter *was* therapeutic. It would cure what ailed you and help you to live longer (I wonder how they conducted their experiments?). I have this bizarre image of old folks gathered in front of videos of Harold Lloyd or Charlie Chaplin, yukking it up. The Director of Therapy announces: "Folks, time for laughter therapy. Please take your seat promptly in the lounge." But suppose Harold Lloyd doesn't seem funny any more? As for Chaplin, his films have been so loaded down with heavy socio-psycho implications by academic cinematographers that there's hardly a laugh left.

A presumably different set of researchers has discovered that it is therapeutic for men to cry. Very briefly: the generation of the Founding Fathers cried publicly and unabashedly. Senators and Congressmen alike wept at Fisher Ames's dramatic defense of the Jay Treaty in 1795 (at least the Federalists did; the Republicans, opposed to the treaty, managed "horrible ghastly smiles"). By the end of the nineteenth century it was considered "unmanly" for a man to weep. The reasons for this dramatic change in what was considered acceptable male behavior are somewhat obscure, but, of course, I have a theory which is sketched out in eight substantial volumes.

In any event, various therapists, not to mention the President of the United States, have made male tears once more acceptable. It is now OK for old men to cry and God knows there is enough to cry about when one considers the ravages of old age, not to mention the condition of the world in general.

Or laugh about. Laughter is essentially social. And infectious. It resounds between friends, especially old friends. One may chuckle alone, but, just as it takes two to tango, it takes two (or preferably more) to create really satisfying laughter. When my wife and I get together with some of our old cronies and we consider the general looniness of the world, we begin to slap our old thighs and cackle and guffaw over the follies and foibles of our species—such as, for instance, Pet Loss Support groups—(uh-oh, here come the letters from the lobbyists for the Pet Loss Support groups); we laugh until we cry and our sides ache. I don't know how it does as therapy. It doesn't seem to help my arthritis and I doubt it will enable me to live to a great old age, but it certainly makes life more rewarding in the meantime.

OLD DANCING

DANCING IS A CLASSIC OLD FOLKS' ACTIVITY. GERALD BONDY WROTE recently that after his wife died he was in despair until he decided to give free rein to his passion for dancing. That opened a new life for him. Now, in his late seventies, he has peaked as a dancer, recently winning *six* "Dirty Dancing" contests in Campbell. Ed Mannion, more sedate, recommends ballroom dancing as the ideal way for an old man to win (and presumably hold) feminine interest.

I am reminded of Samuel Johnson's comment: "There are few things we so unwilling give up, even in advanced age, as the supposition that we still have the power of ingratiating ourselves with the fair sex." Obviously Bondy and Mannion can rest secure in the conviction that they can and indeed do have such a power through the charm of dance.

It works both ways. Old ladies who can kick up their heels can count on the attentions of the opposite sex, and not just fellow oldsters. I am reminded of a conversation I heard several years ago in a bar. There were two young men conversing. It went like this. First young man: "You know Bill's been dating this seventy-year-old dame. I couldn't believe it. He's my age, but I went out with them New Year's Eve and she's not all that bad. She dances good and smells good and she thinks the sun rises and sets on Bill. Now where could you find a twenty-year-old broad like that?" Good question.

A very modest degree of research makes evident that dancing is indeed big with the old. I see in the morning paper that there is a senior dating game "which pairs bachelors and bachelorettes" for "dream dates." A bachelor or bachelorette "will ask questions of potential dates and select a person to go out with. Their dream date will be a night of dancing with Les Brown and his Band of Renown...." I must say, that seems to me going a bit far. This is the old-age-as-farce-school or How To Make Old Age Ridiculous. Les Brown is only one of half a dozen bands that tour the country playing old tunes for old dancers.

The same edition of the paper that notes the "senior dating game" also announces "beginning tap," and "intermediate tap" for oldsters.

Actually, an infatuation with dancing is one of the obsessions that the old share with the young. Statistics (that I have made up) indicate that seventy percent of Americans under thirty "love to dance" while thirty percent of Americans over seventy are similarly inclined.

All of which brings to mind the fact that Americans, Puritans excepted, have always loved to dance. That they loved to dance *more* than their counterparts in other nations (or at least more uninhibitedly) is suggested by the frequency with which visitors to America from the eighteenth century on have commented on our devotion to dancing. In the 1770s Philip Fithian, an English tutor in a Virginia family, noted that Virginians "will dance or die." They preferred "jigs" to waltzes. "Betwixt the Country dances, they have what I call everlasting jogs (to some Negro tune), others come up and cuts them out, and these dances always last as long as the fiddler can play. This is sociable, but I think it looks more like a bacchanalian dance than a polite assembly."

Plantation slaves were as avid dancers as their masters. J.F.D. Smyth, a touring Briton, noted that after an exhausting day's work, a slave danced half the night "with astonishing agility, and the most vigorous exertions, keeping time and cadence, most exactly, with the music of a banjor (a large hollow instrument with three strings) and a quaqua (somewhat resembling a drum), until he exhausts himself...."

Thomas Ashe, traveling in Kentucky in the 1820s, described a "ball" in a tavern. The room, he wrote, was "filled with persons at cards, drinking, smoking, dancing, etc. The *music* consisted of two banjies—crude drums played by Negroes nearly in a state of nudity, and a lute," played by a Chickasaw Indian. "The dancing accorded with the harmony of these instruments....This ball, considered a violent, vulgar uproar by me, afforded the utmost delight to the assembly." Shades of Hard Rock!

When Richard Henry Dana, Boston attorney and author of *Two Years Before the Mast,* traveled on the frontier, he encountered dances everywhere. At one dance, when the fiddler passed out, the "music" was produced by "a tall lad...who bent his knees a little, and began slapping them with the palms of his hands; in two minutes all was going on as merrily as before."

While most young men and women love to dance and many old men and women are equally enamored, they seldom dance together, the most notable exception being the classic American square dance. When I lived in a small New England town in the early 1940s, the weekly square dance at the town hall was the social event of the week. All ages danced together, the young and the old; there the community was reaffirmed and the heart lightened. That was true dancing.

A local character, known simply as Old Uncle Ellis, told Dana that "dancing was the greatest enjoyment of his life, & that a violin set him crazy." A few days earlier, he told Dana, he was driving past a house when he heard a fiddle playing; throwing the reins to a companion "says I, 'Here take the reins, let the horses go to h-ll, I'm going in there,' & I jumped 15 feet, & was in the middle of 'em before they knew the door was open."

There are literally dozens of such accounts all to the same effect: Americans love to dance. In Boston or New York or Fishtail, Montana, dancing has been a favorite social activity for all classes, races, sections, and sexes.

But, by the same token, dancing has always had its critics. In small towns scattered across the country, dancing has been prohibited on the grounds that it resulted in sexual license. In the 1920s, jazz became synonymous for many Americans with decadence, immorality, and disease. The bulletin board at the Albuquerque, New Mexico YWCA listed common venereal diseases and added: "Remember that these diseases can be contracted from kissing or dancing with a man who is diseased....Never forget that at least 25 percent, or one out of every four men you know, are diseased."

In the same spirit, Mrs. E.M. Whittemore calculated that seventy percent of the prostitutes in New York City had been ruined by jazz, in Los Angeles 163 out of 200. In Oshkosh, Wisconsin, a municipal ordinance forbade men and women from "looking into each other's eyes while dancing."

OLD AGE IN THE MEDIA

THE ATTENTION THAT IS CURRENTLY BEING PAID TO OLD PEOPLE IS A mixed blessing. In fact there may be no blessing involved at all. From having been a more or less neglected segment of the population, we now find ourselves center stage. All aspects of the media have a great deal to say about us. Our health, our state of mind, our finances are all subject to incessant comment in magazines, newspapers, film, and TV. Many newspapers have sections devoted to us. We're usually right next to the cooking section.

Needless to say, we appear in a wide variety of guises, the very range of which suggests the profound ambivalence of our society about us. One media category deals with how to look and feel young despite growing old. We see pictures of glamorous dames—not so often gents—who look ten or fifteen years younger than their age. We are told in breathless prose how these miracles are achieved and are encouraged to attempt them ourselves. There are, for example, aerobics for old folks and innumerable other antidotes to aging. The message is clear enough: old age is a desperate state to be avoided as long as possible by all means available. But time, of course, has the last word. Frantic efforts to delay His "winged footsteps," or dissemble His ravages are ultimately futile.

TV ads often depict old men and women as figures of fun, if not of ridicule. Two drawling oldsters promote Bartle and James wine cooler. An ancient dame with a cracked voice parks a monster of a car by knocking two other cars apart to create room for her behemoth. "Where'd you park, Grandma?" an offstage voice inquires. "Right out front." The commercial is for the shorter Honda. Rather stretching the point, I'd say.

Recently, films and TV serieses are making cautious efforts to deal with the theme of old age. The most successful recent effort has clearly been *Driving Miss Daisy. Old Gringo,* starring Gregory Peck as the disappearing writer Ambrose Bierce, was a well-done movie with little box office appeal. A few years ago *Atlantic City,* with Burt Lancaster, was both a commercial and a critical success. All of which is not to mention *Cocoon* and *God* and *God II* with George Burns who has made old age into a road show.

TV has been less successful on the whole than film. There are, of course, "The Golden Girls." They appear to be in their fifties, which is not exactly decrepit, and several of them seem to have little on their minds except sex. Their dialogue is long on innuendo and short on intelligence. They do manage to make the fifties seem funny, but hardly a time of life with any grace or dignity about it. Sophia, the grandmother, is engagingly ascerbic.

"Coming of Age" was a brave attempt to make life in a retirement community hilariously funny, but it only succeeded in making it grim, and its life span was considerably shorter than the average life span in a retirement community.

"Empty Nest" is an engaging tale of a pediatric doctor whose wife has died and who lives with his devoted airhead daughters. He is apparently old enough to retire but since he maintains an active practice of engaging urchins he is doubtless a good role model for older men and women contemplating retirement.

Not only are we a problem, a potential source of humor/entertainment, an economic liability (as we absorb larger and larger portions of the gross national product), we are also a market. In the last analysis, that may indeed be why we are tolerated. The government gives many of us generous subsidies just for being old (and getting out of the way) and, like good Americans, we spend it right and left. We have thus become a target group for advertisers. More and more, TV (and to a lesser extent other media) offers us things devised just for us. Some sticky substance to hold in our false teeth. Cruises, of course, though I confess I never see an old person in the alluring ads that bombard us. The women are lithe young creatures, dancing their heads off; the men are invisible. They are probably all in the bar boozing it up or down in their cabins seasick as dogs.

In a recent sequence of TV ads, a frantically active group of oldsters were leaping about, apparently under the influence of something called Geritol Extend (which, if the antics of the oldsters are any clue, should promptly be investigated by the Food and Drug people). They were guarded against incontinence by a diaper for elders called, appropriately, "Contend." False teeth securely in place, pepped up by Geritol, and wearing Contends, they jumped on motorcycles, yes, motorcycles, and rode off into the Golden Years.

I have the uneasy feeling this is just a foretaste of things to come.

AGE AS PAIN

THE POET W.H. AUDEN WROTE "BELIEVE YOUR PAIN," BY WHICH I assume he meant: Take it seriously. Know that it has a meaning. A purpose. Even a utility. Accept it as an inescapable element of life, especially of later life. I have noted that old age is a pain in the ass and in other parts of the anatomy as well. Mary Holmes and Charles Embree have composed a song on the theme ("My Body Ain't My Buddy Anymore"). Norman Cousins, the advocate of laughing yourself to health, argued that we are a nation of hypochondriacs. And old people, more subject to aches and pains, are worst of all.

There are two common (and usually related) responses to pain. One is to simply withdraw from all actions and activities that produce pain. This is a natural and almost instinctive human (and, for all I know, animal) response. It also means slow death. I have, I think, mentioned that I gave up tennis two or three times because playing increases the pain from my arthritis, and, as I realized later, because I subconsciously assumed that I was getting too old to play. Later, when I realized that getting out of bed in the morning (not to mention walking down stairs) was equally painful, I went back to playing tennis, convinced that the gain was worth the pain.

Another alternative is to run to the doctor for a painkiller. A society dedicated to the pursuit of happiness offers an abundance of drugs to ameliorate pain, relieve stress, bring us down if we're too high up and up if we're too low. We have painless dentistry, why not painless life? I tried that too. Why should I not, after all, have tennis without pain? I was a patriotic American. I had fought and bled for my country and a substantial portion of my pain was related to that fact. My doctor prescribed. That, after all, is his principal function. "Let's try this one first," he said cheerfully, assuring me that there were at least half a dozen others that might prove more efficacious. Fortunately, I suspect, none seemed to really do the trick. Pain came and went in its own unpredictable way. If it went away after popping a pill, I was inclined to attribute the relief to the pill. If the pain didn't go away I took another. And sometimes another.

It was a tedious and often confusing process. Finally, I kicked the pills and continued the tennis.

There is, of course, another way. Or the other way. That is to obey Auden's exhortation: "Believe your pain." Know that it has a meaning. That it anchors you in some mysterious way to life. Americans have never been much good in coping with the darker side of life, with suffering, pain, and tragedy. I remember when I first heard of a young woman disappointed in love who was hustled off by a solicitous mother to a psychiatrist. The mother couldn't bear to see her daughter even temporarily unhappy.

We think of pain as a physical reality and suffering as primarily psychological. Pain-killing drugs are, after all, designed to allay the physical pain; psychiatrists and all the practitioners of the feel-good professions exist to relieve our suffering souls.

The same instinct is evident in both cases. The Constitution or, more precisely, the Declaration of Independence guarantees us happiness (or at the very least holds out the prospect). I suspect many Americans have the vague if inarticulated belief that to be in pain or to be unhappy is unconstitutional.

One notable consequence of the flight from pain is the hypochondria that Cousins writes of. Medical statistics from various industrial nations with comprehensive health care plans for the elderly show that the more health care is available at low or no cost, the more oldsters troop to doctors with inconsequential or imaginary ills. The conclusion is that first-rate health care, the result of humane and enlightened policy, can in fact encourage the kind of consumer mentality which often has a negative effect on the general well-being of the very individuals it is designed to help. Medications become a way of life. This frame of mind—medicate me, please!—encourages self-absorption, one of the principal dangers attendant upon old age. Such self-absorption is often accompanied by what my wife calls "an organ recital," a detailed inventory of the manifold erosions of time.

There is no logic in pain or indeed in suffering. They are not distributed according to any discernible system of punishments and rewards. The good suffer equally with the evil (and sometimes far more). But pain and suffering are woven into the very fabric of life. They cannot be evaded or ignored. They are, in fact, the ground of our humanity. And this is why it is no light matter how we face pain.

I do not wish to be misunderstood. I am no braver than the next man. My inclination is invariably to flee pain and seek ease. The capacity to relieve extreme and disabling pain and, especially, terminal pain is one of the unquestionable achievements of medicine (and not simply modern medicine; ancient medicine knew many potent pain-suppressors). What is at issue, in my opinion, is nothing less than a philosophy of life. So, old friends, tread lightly and believe your pain. And fight it.

WRINKLES

WRINKLES ARE THE INEVITABLE ACCOMPANIMENT OF OLD AGE. WE may hold old age at bay in various ways—jogging, push-ups, dressing and acting young. But wrinkles finally give us away. There are, to be sure, various holding operations—face lifts (I understand men are getting them now), various creams and lotions, injections, even sandpapering and planing the skin, but alas, wrinkles persist.

The unnerving thing about wrinkles is that they come upon you so suddenly. For roughly fifty years or so, allowing for wide individual variations, unwrinkled or only slightly wrinkled, and then wham! You look in the mirror and wrinkles! Almost overnight, serious wrinkles (as contrasted with slight, incipient wrinkles). It's not that wrinkles in themselves are so bad. It is argued, usually by those without wrinkles, that wrinkles give character to the face, an argument not to be treated lightly. If you've lived a happy and fulfilling life, the line goes, you should get good wrinkles, wise little crinkles about the eyes, lighthearted lines about the mouth. I'm not sure that it works that way but it is certainly true that some people, men primarily, look better with wrinkles than without. If foreign movies are an accurate index, European peasants— Spaniards, Italians, Greeks especially—wrinkle splendidly. Same with Mexicans. White American males on the whole wrinkle badly, although there are numerous exceptions. My friend, Al Johnsen, has a magnificent head, perhaps because he is of Viking ancestry. He aged quite early and his head only improves with the years. Visiting New England last month, I saw my dear old friend Bill Martin whom I had not seen in perhaps forty years. He has a magnificent head too, the best, I suspect, on the East Coast.

Wrinkles alone cannot make a great head, of course. There have to be the proper planes and contours for wrinkles to arrange themselves on. Even when one is prepared for or resigned to wrinkles, they can turn up in unexpected places. I don't know quite why, but I found it moderately demoralizing to note that my ear lobes had wrinkled while I wasn't looking. I do not have notable ear lobes and am quite lacking in vanity about them, but somehow it never occurred to me that *they* would wrinkle.

Different parts of the body have different schedules for aging. Benjamin Franklin, in addition to discovering electricity or, at least flying kites, liked to write scandalous little essays. His most famous in this genre is his advice to a young man on choosing a mistress, something every properly (or should we say, improperly) brought up young American in the early days of the Republic was supposed to do (take note of *that* Colonial Dames and Jerry Falwell). When Charles Francis Adams proposed marriage to Abigail Brooks he felt he must part with his mistress. He wrote in his diary: "In the evening I went through one of those disagreeable scenes which occur sometimes in life. No man of sense will ever keep a Mistress. For if she is valuable, the separation when it comes is terrible, and if she is not, she is more plague than profit....What a pity that experience is always to be learnt over and over by each succeeding generation."

Benjamin Franklin urged young men to take old mistresses, partly on the ground that the body aged more slowly in the lower portions; if the head was wrinkled the lover could simply cover it up with a light cloth. An old mistress was, naturally, more experienced. Finally, it was well to choose an old mistress, "because she is so grateful." This is, strictly speaking, a digression, but it is the sort of information about our past that is useful to know lest we think *too* well of our forebears.

Following the Franklin principle, the feet age best of all. Corns and bunions aside, feet hold up remarkably well considering the abuse they are subject to, particularly in the era of jogging. I, for instance, have remarkably young-looking feet. When I feel a bit depressed about the multiplication of wrinkles in the upper reaches I just take off my shoes and look at my young feet. Euphoria! They don't work very well but they look great.

Now all this is, it must be confessed, wrinkles from a masculine point of view. Women clearly take a different view of wrinkles. Beauty and youth typically, at least in our society, are associated. Until relatively recently, the loss of youth was taken to be more or less synonymous with the loss of beauty. Now, we are learning better. There are many celebrated beauties in the public eye, most of them movie or TV queens, women in their late forties, fifties and, indeed, older. But the point is, everyone is entranced less by their beauty per se (I personally think there is nothing more captivating than feminine beauty in the forties and fifties range, unless it be feminine beauty in the teens and twenties) than by the fact that they *look so young!* I suppose it hardly needs be argued that a wrinkle is a far more deadly enemy to a woman than to a man. Most men aren't much to look at to start with and with any luck at all they should improve with age. Henry Kissinger is (or was) said to be quite a hand with the ladies. If Henry Kissinger can play the Lothario almost anything is possible in this mysterious world.

There are certainly beautiful, if wrinkled, old women (one thinks at once of Georgia O'Keeffe), just as there are handsome, wrinkled old men. Maybe the difference is that the beautiful old women are beautiful in spite of their wrinkles whereas the old men are handsome because of their wrinkles.

Then there are jowls but that is another story.

RETIREMENT

GREEDY OLD PEOPLE

I CONFESS TO SOME DISMAY AT THE SIGHT ON THE TV NEWS OF A mob of old folk yowling around House Ways and Means Committee chairman Dan Rostenkowski. It seems they were infuriated by the fact that some million-plus oldsters with incomes in excess of $35,000 a year would have to pay a yearly surtax of $800 for catastrophic illness insurance. Somewhat less than the cost of a cruise for two on a luxury liner.

My dream is that old age in America will one day be viewed as the most fruitful and useful period of one's life—having about it a quality of dignity and even nobility (as it does, of course, in many other societies). But there's not much chance of that, I fear, unless we oldsters get our act together.

We are increasingly seen, by the legislators we petition and harass for more and bigger benefits and by the non-old public, as a selfish interest group hardly to be distinguished from the savings and loan lobby or the champions of a reduced capital gains tax. We appear to believe we are due all kinds of goodies simply because we are old, without regard to need. Admittedly, we have acquiesced to the let's-do-something-nice-for-these-poor-old-folks syndrome: free this, reduced that, ten percent off God-knows-what just because we're over sixty.

Well-intentioned as all this may be, I consider it demeaning. Being old is bad enough without being condescended to every time you turn around. I say, take your damn ten percent. Give me liberty from these patronizing gestures or give me death!

It's these little tips and tidbits, I suspect, that have slowly but surely eroded our consciousness of what old age is, or should be, all about. They've gotten us in our present peculiar frame of mind—the frame of mind that results in our flooding our legislators with mail, most of it selfish and ill-natured.

When there are injustices, let them be remedied, by all means. Where the old are mistreated or exploited, let us defend ourselves. Where the poor old are neglected or in misery, let us help them in the name of charity. But for heaven's sake let us lift our general vision to a somewhat higher plane.

God knows I'm not against agitation, but let's agitate about the things that really count—our insane military budgets, the homeless, the need of young people for affordable housing, the destruction of our environment.

The truth is, each age has its destructive tendencies. With the young it is most often their reckless appetite for experience, their feeling of invulnerability, their scorn for limits and limitations. With the middle-aged it may be a passion for economic security at all costs. Or, for middle-aged men at least, what has come to be known as sports-car menopause, a feeling that their youth is slipping away with a concomitant desire for one last fling.

For the old it is clearly selfishness—a kind of contraction and turning inward, a preoccupation with the processes of erosion, the state of one's kidneys or bowels. What I have referred to often as the "I've done my bit, served my time, paid my dues, now I'm going to indulge myself for a change" approach. Sounds reasonable enough, but in fact it is a premature sentence of death, the foreclosure of an astonishing range of possibilities, of surprises and delights.

It is, in fact, a second childhood. It is the self-preoccupation of the small child who thinks that the world revolves around him, or should. But what is natural to the child and a normal part of her or his development, is corruption in the old, because we know better. Or should.

Much of the blame, of course, can be laid at the door of the wretched retirement business. Retirement almost requires that we meekly adopt a self-indulgent "life-style," that we devote the major part of our time and attention to "amusing ourselves to death" (the title of a recent book on the passion of Americans for entertainment), that we idle away our last days in this vale of tears taking cruises and playing golf.

Marty Knowlton, the founder of Elderhostel, a worldwide program of education for old folks, has founded a nonprofit organization called Gatekeepers to the Future. It is dedicated to "the preservation and restoration of the Earth and all its life." He means to help accomplish this ambitious goal by tapping "the resources, knowledge, skills, wisdom and experience of today's elders...the most experienced group of people the world has ever known." Knowlton sees us as "advocates for the otherwise unrepresented future generations."

He is exactly right. That is, of course, the proper role of the old in any healthy society. They are the testators, endowers, custodians of the future. When old people stoop to being a mere interest group among other clamoring interest groups, beneficiaries rather than benefactors, concerned with themselves and their needs and problems instead of with the world that their grandchildren and great-grandchildren will have to live in, they have turned their backs on their true responsibilities and forgone the principal solace of old age. Most serious of all, they have broken the continuity between generations on which the future of the species, in a real sense, depends.

I don't pretend to speak the last word on the issue of catastrophic illness. Perhaps it does bear too heavily on one segment of the elderly. But in this case we have put our worst foot forward. What is needed is a sea change in the way we oldsters think about our relation to the larger society. To have the respect of our juniors we will clearly have to earn it. We are not doing too well right now.

ONCE I WAS YOUNG
AND NOW I AM OLD

IN THOSE NINE WORDS ARE TO BE FOUND ALL THE STRANGENESS AND poignancy of life. I sometimes have the feeling that the resistance of the not-old to the old, to the vast realm of old age generally, is rooted in a profound reluctance to think about the very nature of existence. Ageism has been added to the list of other "isms" as a form of prejudice against the old in matters ranging from employment to exclusion from various social groups. But ageism, as opposed to racism and sexism, is, in a real sense, prejudice against the future of the self, that is to say, of an individual who with reasonable luck will be old but who is reluctant or unwilling to consider the implications of that fact until it can no longer be avoided. Then it usually comes as something of a shock. Rather than a natural progression, being old becomes a big issue, a problem with, as in the case of all the manifold problems in our society, a host of experts to counsel and advise us on what to do to cope with or triumph over old age (as though, ultimately, that were possible). They distract us (the old) from using old age as a way of coming to terms with, let us say, the meaning of existence.

The old-age-hero, a man more often a woman, who is held up as a model for the rest of us is someone who, despite the onslaught of the years, has remained "young in spirit" or, even better, by, let us say, running in a marathon or doing fifty push-ups every morning before breakfast.

In other words, the often negative response to old people is, as the psychologists like to say, a form of "avoidance," avoidance of the realization of the inevitability of old age and the awesome and fearsome fact that old age is followed by death. Thus ageism is, in the final analysis, avoidance of the most daunting fact of all: we die.

Now we have an industry that is devoted in large part to assisting "old" men and women in avoiding, or obscuring or minimizing the fact of death.

What to do? Is this passion for "avoidance" just another "fact of life," or, more accurately, another fact of life in our particular society? Has any other society in modern or ancient times been as enterprising in suppressing or fuzzing up unpleasant realities?

Why have we, we old people, allowed ourselves to become co-conspirators in this dissembling?

Of course I have that by-now-familiar villain lurking in the wings—retirement. But it is not retirement alone, bad as retirement is for us as individuals and for society as a whole, that is to blame. It is the circumstances under which we retire. Typically, most Americans, especially those of us who "retire," live in cities. By general agreement most cities are, in the most basic sense, unlivable. We need hardly inventory the reasons; we all know them: dirt, crime, disorder, pollution, high rents for poor accommodations, crowdedness, inconvenience on a shattering scale, etc. (San Francisco may be one of the few exceptions among major American cities.) This being the case, as soon as we retire we leave the city to younger and more hardy souls and depart for some sunbelt retreat, some guarded enclave, some distant more or less crime-free small town where the winters aren't too severe. There we gather with aged, middle-class professionals, ex-business executives, ex-airline pilots, whatever subdivision of American human we are most comfortable with—"our kind of people"—the conservative Republicans with the conservatives, the liberal Democrats with others of that vanishing breed. There are preserves even for the old Marxists, speaking of vanishing breeds.

So what's wrong with the perfectly reasonable and rational flight from the city as dominant-American-reality? Given the circumstances, nothing really. But the fact remains that the flight accentuates all the problems inherent in the very notion of retirement. It means literally starting over at a time in one's life when the transition to old age (a very slippery term at best) is, by its very nature, difficult. However enterprising in putting down new roots a retired individual or couple may be, there are in fact no roots like old roots. The city suffers, too, because virtually the only old people left are those rich enough to mitigate the horrors of city life or those too poor or too ill to escape (these latter of course become an additional charge on the strained resources of the city).

My point is that ageism is, in its primary manifestation, an unconscious tactic for evading (or postponing) the ends of life (as well as the end of life) and as such is peculiarly resistant to modification. Racism and sexism are comparatively simple attitudes to change because their negative consequences can be more readily demonstrated.

I found reinforcement for this hypothesis from an unexpected quarter, from Kathleen Woodward, Professor of

English at the University of Wisconsin/Milwaukee. When professors engage "real life" problems, the results in my experience are often disastrous, but Professor Woodward appears to be an exception. In the introduction to her "Aging and its Discontents" she tells of the discomfort of conferees at the annual meeting (1989) of the American Studies Association of France when confronted by a photograph of an old nude male, apparently at death's door. They appeared to be angry with the photographer for "exploiting" the old man but, in Professor Woodward's judgment, they were also "angry at this old man." "In turning away from this particular portrait," Woodward concluded, "it was as if people were turning away from old age itself."

Old age in context, old men and women whom we know and respect or love in the particular reality of their own lives, instruct us in the nature of old age. They are our initiators, our testators. They demonstrate, in their lives, the relationship of old age to the earlier stages of life, by example without didacticism. They lead us toward our own old age, hand in hand. Classically, on the farm, husband and wife *enacted* life from maturity to old age. When retiring city dwellers flee to the country, they have to invent new lives, and those inventions, however ingenious, seldom have the power to enlighten and encourage us in our own quest. They are thus deprived of one of their most essential and rewarding functions. When we look upon them without the ties of kinship or friendship we simply see old men and women, usually not particularly pleasing aesthetically, who, if they register on our consciousness at all, remind us of matters we would sooner forget.

OLD AGE UPDATE

Since I appointed myself an authority on old age I have often thought of Nicolas von Hoffman's prediction some 20 years ago that old age was about to become the "growth industry" of the future. For better or for worse, as a self-appointed authority on old age I attract a good deal of literature on the subject. A lot of firms in the "old age business" send me their publications. These journals and newspapers, which proliferate alarmingly (there is clearly nothing wrong with *their* reproductive systems), find their way to me along with news of various conferences and conventions having to do with "us." I am also regularly informed of freebies and various deductions for the old which on principle I refuse to avail myself of or inform others about, as our would-be benefactors clearly hope.

But I thought I would pass some of the more innocuous items along just in case you've missed them.

The Aging Connection is the "Bimonthly Newspaper of the American Society on Aging," a busy and obviously well-intentioned group, which gives the welcome news that some of the "mature-market" (that's us) magazines have gone the way of all flesh. Prominent among them is *Moxie*, "aimed at the older working woman." She evidently wanted none of it. Magazines aiming at the "mature-market" must follow two basic rules, we are told: be upbeat and don't mention "age" in the title, viz. *Modern Maturity*. The *Reader's Digest* flopped with *50 Plus* and switched to *New Choices* which promptly found six hundred thousand readers. This is peanuts to *Modern Maturity* which has 21.4 million subscribers and bends over backwards to avoid any ads that have a downer quality such as ads for wheelchairs or crutches, anything, indeed, that might make old age seem like what it is, a pain in the ass instead of a prolonged, giddy party.

The Aging Connection is full of information about aging although it has no hints about how to avoid it. Among other things it informs us of the University of Massachusetts' Ph.D. program in Gerontology which promises to bring together "theories, concepts and research methods from several social sciences...." We discover that ageism is on the rise. Complaints about cases of ageism have tripled in the last ten years, thereby keeping pace with sexism and racism. The University of Southern California's Andrus Gerontology Center has responded to this crisis by a developing an "Age Issues in Management" program.

Incidentally, why isn't forced retirement the ultimate example of ageism? Let's run that up the flagpole.

Several books have come to hand recently that deal with various aspects of retirement. First, *Retirement Living*, a comparatively modest volume which is subtitled "A guide to the best residences in Northern California." The editors remind us that in the last century, life expectancy in America has risen from forty-five to seventy-five while the average age at retirement has been "steadily dropping" and now stands at sixty-two. By projecting such figures I can confidently predict that by 2050 our life expectancy will have risen to ninety-two and the average age at retirement will have dropped to forty-five. By 3050 we (not "we" but "they") will live forever: think of the cost of Social Security then!

In any event, our enterprising editors have listed the retirement homes with special attention to amenities which range from golf and swimming to arts and crafts and dancing. We are told whether seats are assigned in dining rooms or seating is helter skelter, the proximity of a doctor or nurse and a beauty parlor, and whether or not the showers have safety bars in them. Clearly, one of the most important items is the proportion of old gentlemen to old ladies (as well as the average age of the residents). At Eden Villa in Castro Valley the female-to-male ratio is four to one and the average age is eighty-five. The residents are described as "quite spry." Some retirement homes accept residents as young as fifty years of age but the average runs more from sixty to sixty-five.

A Field Guide to Retirement is a compendium of things to do and see to ward off the horrors of retirement. For instance, a retiree who wanted some activity to prevent him from becoming a fuddy duddy, built a "turtle complex" which now contains several hundred presumably grateful aging turtles.

The turtle-raiser is overshadowed in my mind by an eighty-nine-year-old Illinois woman known as "Killer" who earned a black belt in the martial art of Tae Kwon Do at eighty-four, and a Saint Paul, Minnesota, retiree who realized her ambition to be "a nun, a bag-lady and a murderess." Stay tuned for the rest of the story.

As the *Field Guide* indicates, there is a disposition to have retirement communities made up of men and women with the same professional and occupational background as "in real life." Thus we have three or four retirement "villages" of ex-army flyers (and Bob Hope Village for retired Air Force enlisted men).

There are numerous denominational retirement communities of course, and Cypress Cove near Kissimmee, Florida, for retired nudists. I personally couldn't imagine a more depressing sight. The older one gets, in my view, the more he/she needs to have old bones covered.

And here's a sobering note. A home in Los Angeles for elderly communists and "social reformers" is being closed. A dying breed?

In addition to hundreds (thousands?) of retirement communities in the United States (the Marriott hotel people, we are told, will build 150 more in the next ten years), there are clusters of American retirees living in foreign countries (where, incidentally, they are at the mercy of fluctuations in the foreign exchange rate). There are thousands in Mexico (Puerto Vallarta is a favorite) and some six thousand in Costa Rica.

So much for retirement communities, at least for the time being. In that happy day when retirement is only an historical footnote there will, presumably, be no retirement communities, just communities.

As part of this update I might mention the latest "scientific research" has confirmed what we knew already, namely that "mentally agile elders [are] as quick-witted at seventy-five as people less than half their age."

This encouraging, if predictable, news comes to us courtesy of a Harvard University study of 1,003 physicians, ages twenty-eight to ninety-two. Not only are the old doctors as "quick-witted," whatever that means (more jokes?), they know a hell of a lot more than young doctors. Specifically, they know a lot more about old age (hence my conviction that they should not be allowed to retire thereby leaving their old patients at the uncertain mercies of young doctors).

Incidentally, I wonder about the new president of Harvard University, whose mother at the age of seventy-seven works in a restaurant (by preference not necessity; when a nosy reporter asked if she intended to continue to work now that her son was president of Harvard, she replied that she had continued to work when he had other jobs and saw no reason to make an exception for Harvard). I wonder if he will stop requiring aged Harvard professors to retire. If aged physicians are as quick-witted as those of their profession half their age, the same should be even truer of aged professors who, it must be assumed, have not had their brains addled by structuralism, deconstructionism, or reconstructionism to the same degree as their younger colleagues ("reconstructionism" is a new movement which I just started and for which I am the spokesperson; its aim is to restore a modest degree of sanity to higher education in the United States).

The fact that the Harvard "researchers" are so surprised at their "findings" brings up an interesting point. Until retirement was invented (very recently, incidentally), people did not regard the old as mentally deficient. Much more commonly the citizenry in general regarded the old as wise. With the imposition of retirement on the society (clearly a consequence of industrial capitalism's notion of obsolete machines and technologies having been applied to human beings), it became necessary to justify retirement by the argument that old (or older) men and women suffered, more or less across the board, from diminished capacity. In a technological society which lives by innovation, wisdom is replaced by knowledge, and yesterday's knowledge is useless.

One of the revelations of the Harvard bunch was that there was no direct or necessary connection between an old man's or woman's physical condition and their mental acuity. In other words, just because the old couldn't walk a straight line (or walk at all) didn't mean they couldn't think straight. The other apparently astonishing discovery (it didn't astonish me, I must say) was that some of the old physicians whose faculties had been rusting away through lack of use over a period of some fourteen years, perked right up when they had some incentive to talk and think, in short, to rejoin the human race.

All, of course, grist for my anti-retirement campaign. Dr. Marcia Weintraub notes, a bit gratuitously I think, that "the brain is like a rubber band." Some people's brains are like "big rubber bands," others have small rubber bands for brains. This seems unjust to Dr. Weintraub, or inexplicable. In a juster world all brains would be the same size rubber bands. I am tempted to say something rude and silly like, "Dr. Weintraub's brain may be like a rubber band but I am confident that mine isn't." But Dr. Weintraub's concern about large and small rubber band brains puts me in mind of William James's comment that as long as one cockroach suffers from unrequited love this is an imperfect world.

Finally, the Harvard researchers take note of the fact that those older physicians who scored in the "top 10" in mental acuity were "far less likely to be retired than their bottom-10 counterparts." Exactly. Stay occupied, stay alive.

An unexpected entry in the gerontology sweepstakes is the Marriott Corporation. Marriott apparently views retirement communities as the housing market of the future. It therefore commissioned the ICR Research Group to find out what we are thinking. Some of the results of the survey are genuine surprises, such as the news that only one-half of Americans sixty-five and over have high school diplomas and only 6.9 percent graduated from college. Eight-one percent of Americans over sixty-five own their own home and ninety percent of those are married. Only seventy percent of those who are widowed or divorced are homeowners and eighteen percent are renters.

Slightly over eighty-two percent of men over sixty-five are married, while only thirty percent of women are; and only eleven percent of men have outlived their wives. Women are three times more likely to be divorced than men (I don't quite understand that statistic) and only four percent of all men and women over sixty-five have never been married (could that be because single men and women die younger than their married counterparts?)

Men and women both declare that they feel younger than their years—men eleven years younger, women thirteen.

One of the more puzzling statistics is that almost half of the men and women over sixty-five polled feel that society treats older people "poorly." Since various surveys purport to show that older Americans (let us by all means avoid that odious word, "seniors") have prospered economically over the last several decades more than any other segment of our society it must be the case that we have a high level of self-pity, or that by the word "poorly" we mean something quite different from a dollars and cents poorly: that we mean treated rather casually, indifferently, patronizingly, or even contemptuously. As though we were no longer of any use to society. As though we had retired.

RETIREMENT

WHEN I ARRIVED IN SOUTHERN CALIFORNIA FROM THE EFFETE EAST forty years ago to try to teach young Southern Californians at UCLA about the New England Puritans, the first question that friendly neighbors asked me was what kind of retirement plan the University had. I had to confess that I had no idea. It had never occurred to me to inquire. I was thirty-five years old, a veteran of World War II, grateful to be alive and to have a job. I was only dimly aware, I suppose, that there was such a thing as retirement. I soon realized that I was in Retirement Land or, as they say, Retirement City. Everyone who wasn't already retired was making elaborate retirement plans ranging from ceaseless motor home travels about the continent to condos in Laguna, La Jolla, or La Something or Other or, for the more affluent, a hideaway in Minorca or an estate in Palm Springs.

If Southern California was then in advance of the rest of the country in its preoccupation with retirement, we have certainly become a retiring nation in the intervening years. We are besieged by retirement plans; retirement communities dot the Sunbelt, the American Association of Retired Persons is one of the most powerful lobbies in the country, and a new category of human beings has been invented called "Senior Citizens." Since Americans seem to have an inherent distaste for calling things by their right name we are always inventing pretentious names for ancient functions or categories. Teen-ager for adolescent, custodian for janitor, sanitary engineer for garbage collector, etc.

Retirement is not, in itself, a particularly encouraging word, suggesting, as it does, abandoning of the field of battle, a move only slightly short of surrender. In a society supposedly committed to the work ethic, our current obsession with retire-ment represents an odd transformation. The fact is that retire-ment is a horrid notion based subconsciously on the idea that people, like machines, wear out and have to be replaced. It encourages a natural disposition in old people to self-indul-gence and self-preoccupation; it accentuates the gap, rapidly becoming a chasm, between the young and the old; it con-tributes substantially to the hardening of arteries, opinions, and joints. It leaves perfectly competent, capable individuals, men especially, at loose ends and underfoot. After the first few months of getting up late, lingering over the morning paper, drinking too much coffee and smoking too many cigarettes, taking the virtually obligatory cruise with hundreds of other members of the "old and restless crowd," playing golf day after day, and visiting the children, there comes a time of despera-tion, a kind of retirement menopause. Some retirees go back to work as consultants, some launch new careers, some (the luckier ones in my view) involve themselves in good causes where their maturity and experience are often invaluable, oth-ers retire to retirement communities to fritter away their time playing bridge, canasta, golf, and bingo.

Among other indignities, retirees have to endure the ignominy of being constantly queried as to whether they are eligible for a "Senior Discount." Certainly the impulse behind the wretched Senior Citizen Discount is a laudable one: Let's be nice to these poor old people, living on dry crusts and pet food, and knock off ten percent (or whatever) from their tickets or their meals. OK, but why should charity stop there? How about single mothers, unmarried mothers, the retarded, the handicapped, the homeless, those on welfare—why shouldn't they have discounts? I always have in my mind's eye the Senior Citizen who drives away from his $350,000 deluxe home (on a golf course, of course) in his Mercedes and has $2.50 knocked off his movie ticket. The Senior Discount is vaguely patronizing and somewhat demeaning as well as thoroughly irrational. Same with Social Security, the current sacred political cow. The country may well sink in a hopeless quagmire of debt but we oldsters, whether we need it or not, are going to cling to our Social Security checks and our Colas. No humanitarian principle is, I trust, better established than the one that says improvident old people should be provided for with some degree of financial security in their more and more extended declining years. Everyone who has paid in over a working lifetime should get back with interest whatever he or she has contributed to the Social Security system but surely those oldsters who are comfortably off should get nothing more. In a modest and admittedly useless gesture, I have taken to refusing Senior Citizen Discounts. "Give it to a single mother," I say to the bewildered ticket-seller.

I had a dream or, more accurately, a nightmare the other night. It was the year 2010 and I was a spry nonagenarian. More than half the nation was retired and the United States was a wholly-owned Japanese subsidiary. There were only two categories of Americans: Seniors and Juniors. The retirement age had been lowered to forty. Cruise lines were overbooked; reservations had to be made years in advance. Some U.S. naval vessels had been turned into cruise liners in response to pressure from the Gray Bears (who counted 150 million members) and the American Association for Retired Persons (with 170 million). Since much power was now solar, many retired oil supertankers had been converted into luxury liners. The huge size of the tankers made it possible to lay out adequate nine-hole golf courses on many ships so that the retired could combine their passion for golf with their addiction to cruises. (It was estimated that at any one time in excess of 10 million Seniors were afloat somewhere.) All available open space in the continental United States had been converted into golf courses, along with some of our best-known national parks, among them Zion, Yosemite, and Yellowstone (Yellowstone was especially popular because of the many natural hazards such as mud holes and boiling springs).

In the final phase of the dream, the outnumbered, but more agile and better-armed Juniors, rose in open rebellion against the Seniors. After a short but sanguinary struggle (many Seniors defended their enclaves courageously armed only with golf clubs), the Seniors were driven from their condos and retirement communities, rounded up on the Seven Seas and forced by the Juniors to go to work to try to help buy the United States back from the Japanese.

I woke up screaming, "But I don't want to work! Don't want to work!" My cries woke my wife, who said tartly, "You never have. Why should you start now?"

It must be said straight out. Unequivocally. Retirement must go. It is an idea whose time has come and gone. A by-product of modern industrial society, it is an anomaly in the so-called post-industrial era. It is based on a faulty concept of human nature and of the relationship of man and woman to the larger society of which they are members. It is inhuman, erroneous, retrogressive, bad for the health and well-being of the retirees, ruinously expensive for the nation, and probably immoral.

Having said all of this, it must, I suppose, be acknowledged that retirement won't be abolished or revised beyond recognition tomorrow. Too many interests uphold it, too many false notions enfold it. Only time, patience, and education will end it. When the child in Hans Christian Andersen's fable cried out that the king had no clothes on, he was, the reader may recall, simply ignored. The procession went on as before. It will probably take a generation or more before retirement, at least as presently understood and practiced, will give way to a more humane and rational view of life. For it is exactly that which is at issue—the nature of existence. As most Americans presently experience it, life in America is made up of three only casually related sequences: childhood (to which is more or less appended teenagehood, formerly adolescence); adulthood; and, finally, old age. As we have noted elsewhere, old age is a vast and on the whole poorly mapped territory, patronizingly referred to (never by me) as Senior Citizen world. Childhod and teenagehood are times of enforced learning, or, since little learning seems to take place, enforced schooling and basic irresponsibility. (It is difficult to recall that in earlier times, fifteen-year-olds sometimes captained seagoing commercial vessels.) Adulthood is a grim period, full of the strain and stress of making a living, getting ahead, raising a family, etc. Rather generally known as Yuppiehood, it is a time, above all, for a wide variety of middle-class therapies designed to mitigate stress, give life meaning, teach "parenting" (yuuck!), and so on. Meantime, adults look forward eagerly to retirement when they can be as irresponsible and self-indulgent as they were in their fondly remembered teens. The lucky ones are double-dippers, those ingenuous enough to enter the last phase of their lives with two or more retirement incomes. But is this life? Two ages of boredom and triviality with a few frantic decades of work sandwiched in between?

The arguments against retirement are manifold, too numerous to mention in a brief compass, but perhaps the most basic is just this point: that every life should have a form and integrity of its own; it should have unity and wholeness. It may encompass half a dozen careers or phases but each phase or career should have some relation to the others. Work and play in some harmonious balance should be characteristic of each phase. It should above all eschew the arbitrary. Mandatory retirement is just such an arbitrary intervention. Obviously not everyone can do every job at every stage of his or her career. There are tasks appropriate to a person at a particular period in life. There are indisputably jobs in which the capacity to perform at high levels of efficiency diminish with age, just as there are many jobs in which experience is more important than stamina or reliability more important than skill. But human performance and the calendar of aging vary so from individual to individual that it is, or should be, impossible to set arbitrary standards. One might, for instance, decide that for a variety of reasons not directly related to physical condition or ability to perform, airline pilots should stop piloting commercial aircraft after fifty-nine, but such a decision should not be characterized as "retirement." Pilots reaching the age of fifty-nine and otherwise in good health should be offered other jobs, one of the most obvious being the training of younger pilots or the opportunity to function as co-pilots or navigators.

There is an ongoing argument about whether retirement is good or bad for one's health. All of us know of tragic cases where someone has looked forward to retirement for years, retired, and died a few years or even a few months later. The proliferating band of experts on old age and aging seem to agree that retirement is dangerous to your health, that individuals who continue to be actively involved, most notably perhaps, artists and performers, are healthier and live longer than those who devote their "golden years" to golf and cruises. If a Casals or a Horowitz retain their remarkable powers into eighties and nineties, why should not the rest of us be as passionately involved in life?

All that is necessary to achieve such a dramatic breakthrough is for us to start thinking differently about life in general. If we are able to think of the kind of life we would like to be able to look back on at the hour of death, we can begin to think of our lives holistically, as we say today.

In more old-fashioned language, we can think of our lives, from birth to death, as our share of God's eternity, and consider how we may be faithful stewards of that gift. That means forgetting about retirement—excising the word from our vocabulary and the practice from our society. Can we seriously question the proposition that we would all be far happier and better off in a society in which all the old too ill or feeble to work were well provided for and all the other old had useful and interesting tasks to perform according to their various and almost infinite capacities? I think we must insist on looking beyond the inhuman, uneconomic, ill-conceived (and recent) notion of retirement to some better day when Americans of whatever age have useful things to do.

Whenever I attack the notion of retirement I am always at pains to state that I am foursquare for providing for those older Americans who for whatever reason are in need of financial assistance. I am also for providing whatever is necessary to ease as much as possible the last stage of our "strange, eventful history," sans almost everything.

The simple fact is that many older Americans have no "safety net" while many others have much more of a safety net than they need. That is to say: our society pays some of us substantial sums whether we need them or not *simply for being old*. As an old person this seems to me absurd. We are told that millions of American children are often hungry to the detriment of their capacity to learn and grow normally.

I am wont (odd word) to stress that the very notion of "retirement" distorts the way we think of our lives in the late industrial world. Or, more specifically, of life itself. Instead of having a kind of unity and coherence, our lives are divided, consciously or unconsciously, into segments: a difficult and problematic youth, a productive period of X years, and *then* this odd finale of an indeterminate number of years when we are turned out to pasture as old delivery horses used to be.

"Research" is constantly discovering what common sense knows: men and women live longer, are healthier and happier, when they have tasks to perform that are compatible with their age and experience.

Whenever I quarrel with the idea of retirement, I get indignant responses from oldsters who tell me about all the interesting and diverting things they do (like running 10 miles a day) in retirement and inform me that they have paid their dues. That strikes me as an odd phrase. What dues and to whom? Is our society some vast disciplinary agency that forces us to undertake tedious and unrewarding tasks in order to put bread on our tables and keep the national economy functioning and then, when we are no longer of use, pays us off? Is existence a kind of involuntary association which requires us to pay dues for the right to live and when we have paid our dues we are then free to amuse ourselves to death?

I suspect that it is indeed the case that many Americans have some such view of life and that it is, typically, based on the fact that they have spent their "productive years" in jobs that they dislike with varying degrees of intensity and from which they can hardly wait to escape via retirement. But I would insist that to view retirement as the cure for the nature of much work in industrial or post-industrial society is to aggravate the problem rather than to solve it. Does it not encourage the attitude that says, "Sure this is shit work but I get to retire in five more years"?

However many golfers or cruisers or joggers retirement produces, the simple fact remains that retirement as it is presently perceived is an economic drain on our society and an enormous psychological hazard for most of those individuals who "retire"—much more so for men than for women, the "researchers" tell us (and common sense does too).

In my view, the fact that we are so frequently edified by accounts of men and women who *despite being retired* have found ways to live useful and rewarding lives is the best indicator of the absurdity of the whole institution of retirement.

THE OLD AGE SURTAX

As I HAVE NOTED FROM TIME TO TIME, ONE OF THE PARTICULAR hazards of old age is selfishness and self-absorption, the tendency to, like the children we once were, place ourselves, our appetites, and concerns, in the center of the universe. Excusable and indeed inevitable as this impulse may be in children, it is the least attractive quality of old age.

Our feel-good society, determined to exploit us elders in every conceivable way (under the guise of kindly interest) is constantly urging us on to new heights (or depths) of self-indulgence.

A publisher just sent me a work entitled alluringly "Freebies (& More) for Folks Over Fifty." It tells us what great fun it is to get old. We are to be rewarded for our good fortune in reaching the age of fifty (there they go again, lowering the threshold of old age in order to pick our pockets a bit earlier) by a veritable cornucopia of goodies. "The two most important questions to ask, now that you're part of the mature market, are..." (certainly not the meaning of life or how to face old age with some dignity or how to find a useful role to play in your latter years but, listen closely): "'Do you have discounts for seniors?' and 'What is the lowest available rate?'"

We are enjoined to "Memorize these questions and use them everywhere you go to purchase products and services."

I have been hard at work memorizing them. "Do you have discounts for seniors?" I write each query down dozens of times until I have it firmly fixed in my mind because I am assured that when I have accomplished this I will have "entered into a new life and a new world," a world of panhandling ancients announcing to every vendor, "here I come, gimme my ten percent" (or more).

Whenever I talk this way, I enrage many of my coevals. They accuse me of being a hard-hearted Scrooge determined to snatch the dry crust of bread from the mouths of poor old people. The fact is that there are many older citizens, especially those who belong to one minority or another, who have not shared in the general economic elevation of most oldsters. I cannot say too often that this situation seems to me intolerable, one that must be remedied (as must the fact that some thirty million Americans do not have adequate health care). But poll after poll professes to find that what are essentially middle-class American oldsters have benefited disproportionately in the last few decades. While more and more children fall below the poverty line, more and more old men and women go on cruises. With those older Americans who by their labors have amassed the wherewithal which enables them to idle their last days away I have obviously no argument. That's their own decision, foolish as it may seem to me. All those old men and women who have paid into the Social Security fund during their working years *should get back what they have invested whether they need it or not.* But I cannot understand the logic or the principle of social justice that continues to endow them after it has repaid them and in so doing places a heavy economic burden on the rest of society. We have an enormous budget deficit and an almost incomprehensible national debt. Yet any suggestion that this burden be shared in some equitable way by the vastly growing legion of the prosperous old is greeted by howls of indignation. Addicted to freebies of every conceivable kind, we demand our governmental freebies stridently and persistently. After all, if we are to "have the time of our life in the prime of our life" (roughly the period from fifty to ninety) we need every dime we can get our clutches on.

We are presently in one of our deeper recessions since World War II. Millions of Americans are out of jobs, many faced with the loss of their homes. Our inner cities are in an advanced state of decay. Millions of those Americans lucky enough to have jobs complain of the stress that results from holding down a job in the late-twentieth-century U.S. And what about us? Well, we are making desperate efforts to entertain ourselves in a society where entertainment doesn't come cheap. Perhaps there is something we could do to help our fellow Americans, among them our own children and grandchildren, rather than increasing the drain upon them. Since it is such a blast being old, shouldn't we be willing to pay for the privilege? I suggest that if all of those who didn't need that wretched ten percent contributed it to a national fund, a good deal of folding green would accumulate to be used at our discretion for the benefit of those in our society who need it most. This idea didn't seem to catch on. So I have a better idea. Those of us fortunate enough to have achieved this blissful state of being old should be willing to pay for its advantages in the form of an "Old Age Surtax," a ten percent levy on every old man and woman, or couple over fifty years of age with incomes over, say, forty thousand a year, adjustable for regional living costs.

As for all those well-intentioned people determined to batten off us, I have two words only: "Get lost."

DEATH

Thinking about Death

Death is substantially more certain than taxes. The fore-knowledge of our own death, it has been said, is what distinguishes us from animals. Death is everywhere in life and although we all know that we must die, on one level we do not believe we will. What we know with our conscious minds our subconscious denies. While reason and experience of the deaths of friends and loved ones tell us that we cannot live forever, unreason whispers that we will not die. Such is the power of being, it is very difficult to imagine a state of non-being. One "authority" on death (can there truly be such a thing?) has written, death is "the most mysterious, the most threatening, the most tantalizing of all human phenomena." Who would dare argue the point?

The young and the old think more about death than those in between who are apt to be far more caught up in the immediate pressing concerns of making a living and raising a family. The young are so full of life that death is a chilling thought. When I was eighteen I wrote a typical eighteen-year-old's poem on death that ended:

Who in a hundred years will think of me?
My loves, my joys, my sorrows,
Where will they be?
How like the ant

I build my mound of sand
For time to brush aside with thoughtless hand.

The old think of death because it is near. I suspect that a good guidepost to the country of the old comes when we begin to calculate how many more years we may, with reasonable luck, expect to live. Mother lived to—was it seventy-six or seventy-seven? Father a year or so longer. Grandfather to seventy-seven, Grandmother to eighty. I'm sixty, or sixty-five, or whatever age. Without some catastrophic illness my life expectancy therefore should be, say, seventy-five to eighty. With some luck and since everyone seems to be living a bit longer these days, eighty or even eighty-five. That's the way old people think. On a more practical level: "Am I buying my last suit or car?" "Will I be here to ride my mare's foal by the time it is fully grown? Should I breed my mare?" "Will the tree I plant bear fruit when I am still around to enjoy it?" Such thoughts are not necessarily morbid. They are simply common sense. One watches the obituaries to be informed of the death of friends and contemporaries and also to satisfy a morbid curiosity over the ages at which people seem to be dying and the causes.

We make much of (and presumably derive much satisfaction from) the fact that "life expectancy" is much greater today in America than it was a hundred years ago. But statistics are misleading. In the nineteenth century the average life expectancy was much reduced by the high rate of infant mortality and the deaths of children. The rigors of constant childbearing brought many wives to early graves and many occupations were hazardous in the extreme (the life expectancy of iron and steel workers, for example, was forty-one and forty-three years respectively). But many Americans, especially those of the middle class, lived as long or longer than their present-day counterparts. This was notably true of reformers and politicians. John Adams lived to his ninetieth year. Jefferson died in his eighties, Charles Carrol of Carrolton, one of the signers of the Declaration of Independence, lived to ninety-five. Pierce Butler, a member of the Constitutional Convention from South Carolina, died at the age of seventy-eight. John Jay, first Chief Justice of the Supreme Court, lived to eighty-four. Reformers were as long-lived as Revolutionary statesmen. Harriet Beecher Stowe was eighty-five when she died. Her sister, Catharine, was seventy-eight. Margaret Sanger, the champion of birth control, eighty-four; Sojourner Truth, the great black abolitionist preacher, eighty-six; Susan B. Anthony, eighty-six; Victoria Woodhull, the advocate of Free Love and indeed every radical cause, eighty-nine. (The obvious moral: if you wish to live a long (and useful) life, become a reformer; it is excellent for one's health.)

The point of all this is that the old are very conscious of, if not preoccupied by, death. When you are old you assume a different relationship to your body. If you are a young athlete, for example, your body may be your fortune. Some young people seem to be in love with their bodies; certainly they display as much of them as the law allows, and occasionally more. When you are old your body becomes in a sense your enemy. In spirit, in essence, you feel as young as ever but your body constantly reminds you otherwise. Young as you may feel, you know that someday, somehow, your body will do you in. If your body were more cooperative there is no telling what prodigies you might perform. If it did not go on decaying around you like the outworks of some once-impregnable fortress, you could live forever. The body becomes an early warning system: a suspicious pain here, an unsightly discoloration there may portend the beginning of the end. Your body becomes a messenger with unwelcome news.

I don't wish to overstate the case but there is clearly no evading it. You are inclined to say to your body when it begins to fail you, "After all that we've meant to each other, why does it have to end like this?"

While a reasonably lengthy old age allows one to prepare for death (so far as that is possible for anyone much attached to life), compose one's spirit, rearrange the past to one's satisfaction, and put one's present affairs in reasonable order, there is still the troublesome question of when the hour cometh. John Adams, defeated as President of the United States in the election of 1800 by his one-time friend, Thomas Jefferson, returned to his beloved Braintree to put his affairs in order and die. He lived an unexpected (and to some degree unwelcome) twenty-six more years.

So suppose you get everything in order for the end, and find yourself with twenty or twenty-five more years on your hands. You can't play golf *all* that time. That is the dilemma of so-called retirement.

The philosophical point I would like to make is that of my mentor, Eugene Rosenstock-Huessy. Since we do not know the day or manner of our demise, we should try to live life backwards from death. At the beginning of life's journey, Rosenstock-Huessy argued, we should attempt to imagine ourselves at the end of life and ask from that final perspective how we would like to have lived our lives. How would we wish to be known, however modestly, to our posterity?

OBITS

I get up each morn and dust off my wits,
Pick up the paper and read the obits;
If my name is missing, I know I'm not dead
So I eat my breakfast and go back to bed.
Courtesy Tanner Wilson

I DON'T KNOW WHETHER IT'S SIMPLY ME OR OLD MEN IN GENERAL who turn with a kind of morbid fascination to the obituaries. Even before the sports pages. Do old women have the same proclivity? Based on my wife, I suspect not. She's contemptuous of my preoccupation with the obits. For me they are a kind of vivid daily reminder of my own mortality (as if I needed any reminders). The age of the deceased is the principal object of my attention. There seem to me to be odd groupings, age-wise, as they say. Some days a disproportionate number of those who have died will be in their sixties. Other days the eighties are heavily represented. And, scattered here and there, the real tragedies of our time, young men who have died of AIDS. I am curious about the causes of death. "After a long illness" is the most chilling, summoning up as it does the image of grim years in retirement homes. In our local paper there is often a puzzling reticence about the cause of death. But there are usually clues such as "contributions to hospice [cancer probably] in lieu of flowers" or to the Heart Foundation or Stroke Center.

I am curious about the usually meager details of the careers of the deceased in the obituaries. First, his or her occupation. Ministers seem to live, for example, longer than lawyers. Hard physical labor, so praised and exalted by those who don't do it, usually shortens life. Steelworkers don't live as long as teachers, generally speaking.

Survived by children, grandchildren, great-grandchildren, living where? If in the community where the deceased lived, one summons up a picture of a large, close-knit family. And if the offspring have scattered, where have they scattered to?

Compressed into each modest obituary, a dozen or so lines, is not simply one life but many. Each obituary is like a condensed novel. One longs to probe its multiformity, how in one degree or another it recapitulates the story of the race.

I suspect the questions of how long we may expect to live and how we shall die are among the most basic preoccupations of the species, especially when we are conscious of having run by far the better part of the course. I search the obituaries for clues. Of course, they are not really there, extrapolate as one will. Each life has its own unique shape, meaning, and end. Yet there are often tantalizing uniformities. The display of what I have called the survivalist syndrome is not a very laudable but, I suspect, a very human impulse. When you read of those who have died younger than you presently are, you feel a slight, rather shamefaced satisfaction in having lived a bit longer as well as a pang for the individual. One is reminded of what is perhaps life's greatest inequity, that many people die "before their time."

It seems to me that the guilt-tinged response to obituaries points to a larger phenomenon: the old feel a bit superior to those who are not as old as they. Thus the seventy-year-olds regard the sixty-year-olds as still wet behind their ears. The seventy-five-year-olds patronize the seventy-year-olds and on up the line. To the eighty-five-year olds, the sixty-five-year-olds are just kids and there is often a good deal of banter among oldsters revolving around the difference in their ages (whereas, of course, to the young, anyone over fifty seems ancient).

The subtle and considerable gradations that the old are themselves so conscious of correspond to a reality. Old age does unfold, with any luck, as a series of minor (and sometimes major) revelations. My friend Edward Gans is over 100 years old. The last decades of his life have brought him a succession of "miracles."

Recently someone told me of an old relative who was pleased to reach ninety because, he said, he noticed that very few people died in their nineties.

And then, of course, there's one's own obituary to consider. I seldom think of obituaries without recalling an experience with my own. I was doing a piece of writing for *Time-Life Books*. One of the editors was showing me around. As we passed a section of the larger Time-Life library, I noted a room full of manila folders. What were they? I asked. It was the morgue where they kept information on almost everybody so that their demise could be noted in *Time*. There's probably one there on you, she said kindly. When I expressed doubt that anyone as obscure as I could be in so elevated a spot (it was on the fifteenth floor as I recall), the editor assured me that there were people even less worthy of note than myself there.

Would I like to look? I found the idea irresistible. She searched and there I was. When she opened the folder, the top item was from a gossip column and read something like this: "Page Smith is marrying Boopsie Playgirl of Southampton. They will go on a safari in Kenya for their honeymoon. Smith, a professor of history at UCLA, has four children by an earlier marriage." I recalled the item. The columnist, assuming quite naturally that there could hardly be more than one Page Smith on the planet, had confused me with a high-flying airline pilot of the same improbable name. I was (and am) still blissfully married to the mother of our four children. Fortunately I had lived long enough to repair the error, but it imbued me with a degree of skepticism about all obituaries, my own included.

Death Rehearsal

Sidney Smith, the English essayist, wrote in 1836 in a letter to a friend: "One evil of old age is that, as your time is come, you think every little illness is the beginning of the end. When a man expects to be arrested, every knock at the door is an alarm."

Recently, due to a breakdown in communication between my doctor and myself, I interpreted a summons from him as the call of the Grim Reaper himself. I had several days before my examination was scheduled to think about THE END. I tried various approaches to buck myself up for the anticipated verdict. I had had, I assured myself, a very interesting and rewarding life (due, in large part, to my interesting and rewarding wife). My financial affairs were in reasonably good order, the mortgage was paid off, there was a little money in the bank; the interesting and rewarding wife had an assured if modest income. I had finished (and published) the only book I had in mind. I had just mended the fence around the horse pasture. I had long ago, albeit grudgingly, accepted the fact that I could not really expect to live forever. And I had attempted to persuade myself that that being the case, the seventies were not bad time to cash in one's chips. After all, the Psalmist reminds us (Psalm 90): "The days of our years are threescore and ten; and if by reason of strength they be fourscore years, yet is their strength labor and sorrow; for it is soon cut off and we fly away." Henry Wadsworth Longfellow compared reaching the age of seventy to climbing the Alps. The valley stretches behind you, and ahead lie "other summits, higher and whiter, which you may not have the strength to climb." Longfellow's friend, Oliver Wendell Holmes, had the encouraging thought that "to be seventy years young is sometimes far more cheerful and hopeful than to be forty years old."

As a close reader of obituaries, I found myself fretting over the possibility that mine might omit my five years of service in the Army of the United States in World War II and at least a passing reference to my Purple Heart.

And no eulogies. Just the grand cadences of the Burial of the Dead in the Book of Common Prayer: "Man, that is born of woman, hath but a short time to live, and is full of misery. He cometh up, and is cut down, like a flower; he fleeth as it were a shadow, and never continueth in one stay.

"In the midst of life we are in death; of whom may we seek for succour, but of thee, O Lord...."

In any event, I totaled up the reasons why I should be quite reconciled to my demise and meet, if not exactly greet, it with dignity and resolution. They made an impressive total. Moreover, death is, after all, what life is finally all about.

All of this worked only partially. If I was ready for the Big D, why did I wake up in the middle of the night in a cold sweat and my breakfast taste like ashes in my mouth?

As it turned out I had misinterpreted my summons. It was all a routine matter. I was going to live for an indeterminate period longer.

Seeking to extract something positive from my clearly temporary reprieve, it occurred to me that such alarms, coming every few years, might serve the purpose of getting a person in psychological shape for the ultimate bad news, rather like an athlete doing push-ups and windsprints prior to the big event. After all, facing death with equanimity is the final and perhaps most estimable act in life.

BIRTHDAY MEDITATIONS

HAVING RECENTLY PASSED MY SEVENTY-FIFTH BIRTHDAY, I HAVE BEEN moved to reflect on the significance of this modest (but certainly welcome) degree of longevity. The only immediate benefit that I can discern in reaching the not-very-honorary age of seventy-five is that I can be mildly patronizing to those friends and acquaintances who are only seventy-four. That is a game that old people play. Seventy-five-year-old to seventy-four-year-old: "Well, young feller, how are you today," etc.

The fact is that the passage of the latter years is discernibly different from the passage of other years, the years of youth or middle age. Whatever else may or may not be true, you are undeniably one year nearer the end. The fact that the end is uncomfortably near is borne home most poignantly by the deaths of friends and/or relatives and, in a somewhat different fashion, by the deaths of celebrities that one identifies with one's youth. Such deaths are somehow more unsettling than the deaths of older people we know. The Rita Hayworths and the Irene Dunnes live in our memories forever young and charming. It is thus disconcerting to be reminded that they became old ladies who aged just like the rest of us, but offstage, so to speak.

Being seventy-five, I recalled my sixty-fifth birthday in 1982, when I became old. Things were difficult for a time.

One wanders into old age like someone lost in a forest with no clear paths or guidelines other than an endless prospect of golf and cruises.

At sixty-five everything suddenly seemed quite problematical. A certain heaviness fell upon my limbs. I gave up tennis on the assumption that I was now too old to play. Anticipating fatal illnesses in every unfamiliar ache or pain, I trotted off to my increasingly impatient doctor. It gradually dawned on me that early old age was, in practical fact, no different from late middle age. My spirits revived. I took up tennis again. After wearing glasses for forty-some years I took them off one day and found I no longer needed them. That was perhaps the most encouraging episode of my first year of being old. I had, briefly to be sure, the illusion that like my dear friend, Bert Kaplan, I was getting younger while growing older.

Now, years later, I am pretty relaxed about being old but more conscious than ever of what a strange stage of life it is and how constantly one's perceptions of old age shift.

We oldsters have a disposition, I suspect, to develop a kind of survivalist mentality as though simply living a long time were some kind of achievement. At some point we begin to hoard the years, putting each one away with a little pat of satisfaction. "There you go, number seventy-two. Thought you had me, didn't you?" I suppose this is all harmless enough as long as you don't let it get out of hand.

Incidentally, I wonder, with the end of the Cold War, what has happened to the other survivalists, those grim warriors who, in anticipation of a nuclear Armageddon, have armed themselves to the teeth, laid away great stocks of food, and prepared to withdraw to underground refuges, planning, when the holocaust was spent, to emerge, shoot any liberal Democrats who may have survived and take over whatever might be left of the world? What are they up to now?

It is also, I reflect, odd to be growing old with the century. Since medieval times, the ends of centuries have brought a great variety of malaises, chief among them what we might call the end-of-the-world blues, marked by beards and long hair on men and a general relaxation (if that is the proper word) of social standards and, perhaps most notably, sexual mores. Suicide especially has been associated with end-of-the-world blues and, of course, the rise of strange cults and mysterious religions. We are determined to anticipate an end to the world, in addition to the end of the century. Now that the chances of a nuclear holocaust seem more remote, we are scaring ourselves to death with the destruction of our environment.

In any event there is, from the perspective of seventy-five years, much wrong in the world, much wrong, heavens knows, in our dear United States, and, not by any means least of all, much wrong with being old in the United States. But there is also ground for hope. I believe a day will come when compulsory retirement is judged unconstitutional, when older men and women (no longer a burden to society and themselves) are productively employed in jobs suitable to their experience and rated to their physical capacities, and, most important of all, are not pitied and patronized but respected for, if not their wisdom, then the living they have come through and what it has taught them that needs to be passed on to successive generations.

FAMOUS LAST WORDS

At my yearly medical check-up the other day, my peppy, preppy young doctor asked me to fill in a sheet headed "Final Care." It had to do with my last wishes. I was supposed to check one of several alternatives for my final hours in this vale of tears. Under "Unlimited Care," it read: "Even if I have to spend the rest of my life attached to a respirator or other machine, keep me going *by any means available.* Quit only when my mind is completely gone." That sounds rather like stacking the cards to me. Would anyone check number one?

The other choices were a bit less hairy. Number three reads "I am ready for death now. If I become critically ill, I don't want any cures. Just keep me comfortable and let me die with a minimum of fuss." That seemed pressing things a trifle. "I am ready for death now"? Did the doctor mean *right this minute?* Was he not telling me something I might not want to know?

It set me to thinking.

In the nineteenth century, Americans had what would seem to us today a morbid preoccupation with death (small wonder—it was omnipresent from consumption, diptheria, smallpox, and a variety of other usually fatal diseases). A classic example of morbidity is the case of the great painter of the era of the American Revolution, John Trumbull, who painted his wife dying. Since death was such a closely observed event, people gave a good deal of thought to the manner of their demise, particularly their last words. Many last words have such a ring of eloquence about them that it is hard to believe they hadn't been thought up ahead of time. Some, though, were undoubtedly spontaneous. Stonewall Jackson, fatally wounded and delirious, said, "Let us cross the river and rest under the shade of the trees," or words to that effect. John Quincy Adams, serving in Congress after he had been defeated for a second term as President by Andrew Jackson, fell to the floor of the House from an apparent stroke. Briefly revived, he said, "It is finished; I am content," which seems to me a wonderful exit line.

A great-uncle of my wife is remembered in the family for his last words: "I have lived a blessed life." My mother, among her last words, said that she had had a happy life. Although her life seemed a hard and often unhappy one to me, it was vastly cheering to hear her say that it had been happy and to hope that I may have contributed to that happiness. That was doubtless what she had in mind; she was thoughtful and generous in death as she had been in life.

Not infrequently, last words were used to extend a tyranny over the living from beyond the grave, i.e. "Promise me, dear, you'll never take a drink of whiskey. Your poor father was a drunkard." Or smoke. Or remarry. To the latter request from a dying husband in colonial times, the wife is said to have replied (in verse): "From this vow I beg you'll me excuse / For I'm already promised to John Hughes."

My doctor's query about "Final Care" got me to thinking about *my* last words. If you fall down dead from a stroke that, obviously, is that. No last words. If you're attached to a machine and barely conscious, ditto. But if you're lucky enough to expire full of years and God's good gifts with your children, grandchildren, etc., gathered around your bed, then, it seems to me, it would be nice to have a good curtain line handy and this obviously requires some forethought (or a good ghost writer). Something wise or encouraging or, perhaps, witty *and* wise. Something to remember me by. (A friend's grandmother made him sing with her, "Now is the hour, the hour when we must part." A bit too sentimental I'd say, although he apparently took it in good spirit.)

I wonder if it would be considered plagiarism to use somebody else's last words? Perhaps one should then say, "In the words of John Quincy Adams, 'It is finished...'." Or, "As my great uncle Abercrombie said... 'So long. Good luck'." (Much too banal.)

The problem is that in order for your last words to be famous, *you* have to be famous, which rather complicates things. In poking through famous last words I haven't found any that were famous despite the fact that the speaker of them was obscure. A retired postal clerk in Fishtail, Montana, is not going to be remembered for his last words, however striking. It seems to me unfair that you have to be famous to begin with in order to be credited with famous last words. It casts a shadow over the whole enterprise. Maybe the proper thing to do is to die in decent, resigned silence, keeping one's final thoughts to oneself.

A safer, if less dramatic and memorable, alternative would be to deliver such sentiments well in advance of the last hour. Or leave a letter marked, "To be opened on the occasion of my death," just like in old-time movies. Anyway, it's worth thinking about. I guess.

LIVING AS LONG
AS YOU EXPECT TO

MY FAVORITE HUMORIST, ART HOPPE, RECENTLY NOTED A STUDY BY a psychologist that reported to show that, taking one thing with another, people lived *as long as they expected to live,* a fascinating if dubious proposition. Hoppe went on to observe that he had always expected to hit the wall at age fifty-eight but having survived that age by some five years, he was now ready to entertain the psychologist's notion that he had only to anticipate a more advanced age to have a reasonable assurance of reaching it. He had chosen ninety. Certainly a good round age. I think I'd settle for eighty-five. The real issue, of course, is not age but condition.

In any event, Hoppe's column set me to thinking about one's "target age," if that is the proper expression.

My experience is that it keeps shifting. I recall that Lincoln Steffens, in his famous autobiography, mentions that his first wife devoted most of her time to caring for her ailing mother. Then Steffens's wife discovered that she herself had a fatal illness and had only a few months to live. She had sacrificed her own interests and pleasures—her own life—to her mother's needs, confident that after her mother's death she would be able to live fully. Faced with the fact that she was destined to pre-decease her mother, she was furious.

I also recall the comments of an old friend from my army days. He was the son of immigrant Italians. His father had worked in a shoe factory. An early death was the typical fate of those immigrants like his father who worked long hours at exhausting jobs. My friend had two ambitions: he wished to be an officer in the United States Army and to live to the age of sixty-five. When I saw him last he was a retired lieutenant-colonel and had reached seventy. He was plainly delighted.

I myself have been inclined to measure my life in terms of the time required to finish a current book. When I was working on my first substantial literary project, a biography of John Adams, the second president of the United States, I began to feel poorly. Being of a somewhat morbid turn of mind, I at once assumed I was suffering from a terminal illness that would prevent me from completing what I then considered my magnum opus. The biography took on for me the character of a race with death (I was then forty-three). It turned out there was nothing more seriously wrong with me than a case of hepatitis. I completed the manuscript with a feeling of triumph but then came the Cuban missile crisis. Just my luck, I thought: World War III is going to break out, we'll all be annihilated and my book will never be published.

The disposition to measure out my life in book-long spans remained. I was strongly conscious of it as I began a multi-volumed history of the United States. Started, for all practical purposes, in 1978 when I was sixty-one, the undertaking consumed much of my time and energy for the next eight years. Demanding as it was, I survived; indeed it gave me a new lease on life. When the history was finished I swore off any subsequent books, perhaps with the subconscious feeling that since I had been spared to complete the history I shouldn't push my luck.

The point of all this is that I suspect many men and women as they get older, rather than expecting to live for a specific number of years, are inclined to take old age in segments. Pleased at making sixty-five, they decide to try for seventy. Having made seventy, how about seventy-five? If you have it firmly set in your mind that you intend to live until you're eighty-five, say, and, the vicissitudes of life being what they are, you realize at sixty-five or seventy or seventy-five or even eighty that you are not going to reach your target age, the feeling may be one of considerable if not acute disappointment. Whereas if you take life one increment of time—one interesting task or a modest number of additional years—at a time, when the Big D comes you're not so apt to feel let down.

As I approach my middle seventies they don't (or I don't) seem old at all! I am disconcerted to realize how old that seemed to me when I was in my middle sixties. I remember attending friends' seventy-fifth birthdays, astonished that they could still get around.

Despite our psychologist's "finding" that people generally live as long as they expect to live (how, incidentally, do you suppose he found that out?) I am going to take it one year at a time, keeping in mind the fact that I was delighted to have survived my forty-third birthday and pleasantly surprised to have been spared to finish my history. Anything beyond seventy seems to me a bonus.

Meantime, I take comfort from a poem of Robert Herrick, the Puritan divine, who wrote in 1648:

Young I was but now am old,
But I am not yet grown cold;
I can play, and I can twine
'Round a virgin like a vine:
In her lap too I can lie
Melting, and in fancy die:
And return to life, if she,
Claps my cheek, or kisseth me:
Thus, and thus it now appears
That our love outlasts our years.

FAVORITE EXITS

ONE OF "RIFF CHARLES" EMBREE'S SONGS ENDS:

I'll tell you thus, my pretty frail,
Each of us owes God a death
And the check is in the mail.

The older one gets the more conscious one becomes that the check is not only in the mail, the delivery date is getting closer. This thought in turn is apt to direct our attention to the nature of our exit. The least desirable end is one that involves being kept going by some life-support system long after there is any hope of recovery. This is hard on everyone concerned and has led to the sensible notion of life wills wherein the prospective deceasee can assert his/her unwillingness to be kept alive by such desperate measures.

What brought this mildly morbid line of thought to mind was a recent letter from a friend who wrote that until recently he had thought that the preferred, if not ideal, way to kick off would be to be "alone in a duck blind, surrounded by the sights and sounds of the marsh." I assume that my correspondent is an avid duck hunter. His prescription, I must say, leaves me cold, both figuratively and literally. Although I have never shot ducks, my image of a duck blind is of an extremely chilly spot, ducks or no ducks.

As for myself, my preferred exit activity would be trout fishing and the ideal locale, the braids below Ennis on the Madison River. But any high-class trout stream would do. Second, I suppose, would be the tennis court, just after putting away an ungettable overhead shot.

There are certainly places where one would not wish to be found dead. The father of a friend of mine, a gentleman of the cloth, incidentally, checked out in a house of ill-repute. The fact that it was a high-class house may or may not have been a comfort to friends and family, not to mention members of his congregation.

My correspondent confesses that he has never been able to bring himself to indulge his secret desire to see a XXX-rated movie "by the semi-conviction that if I did so, it would be there that I would meet my doom from an earthquake, heart attack, stroke, fire, or falling chandelier." It seems a shame for him to miss out on one of the most notable aspects of our culture through simple cowardice. Or prospective post-mortem uptightness. Couldn't he just rent an X-rated home video?

In any event, my friend seems much too ready to abandon his hope (certainly it can be no more than a hope) to cash in his chips in a duck blind simply because the father of one of his friends died in a blind during a duck hunt and the whole thing turned out to be somewhat of a hassle, a strain on those who had to "extract him from the blind (which is a large barrel sunk nearly to its edge in water)." Come on, I know *that much* about hunting ducks! "All very damp and messy and undignified...a terrible imposition," my correspondent concludes.

Imposition, my foot! What are friends for?

Catching Up

ONE OF THE ODDER EXPERIENCES OF OLD AGE IS CATCHING UP WITH one's parents. What happens often is a strange merging of generations. When you are young your parents seem old to you, even though they may in fact be quite young. When you are in your late thirties or early forties and they are, let us say, in their sixties, it may occur to you that they are not so old after all. Indeed, as both you and your parents get older, the difference in your ages diminishes, not absolutely of course, but relatively. In other words, when you are a ten-year-old your parents may be in their mid-thirties and thus three-and-a-half times as old. But when you are forty and your parents are, for the sake of argument, sixty-five, you are only eight thirteenths (is that right?) of your parents' age and gaining all the time.

If the mother makes it to one hundred and the daughter to seventy-five (which sometimes happens), the daughter will be three-fourths of her mother's age. (It works equally well, if more rarely, with sons). From having been, at one year of age, one-twenty-fifth of her mother's age, the daughter is now *almost* the same age. Frustrating to get so close but how strange to get close at all!

Seen another way, the "catching up" phenomenon is a commentary on the oddness of the category "old" and the extraordinary range of life experience that it covers.

I hesitate to mention the "catching up" phenomenon for fear some gerontologist will fasten on it and make it the subject of a study or survey, but I will offer a few observations of my own in any event. My mother-in-law lived to ninety and it was fascinating to me to observe how the relationship between her and my wife changed in the last decade of her mother's life. From having surrendered supervision and control over my wife many years ago and good-naturedly acquiescing in our way of bringing up her grandchildren, she gradually became more assertive and demanding. She did not hesitate to criticize my wife's manner of dressing, or the dishes she cooked for her, or her opinions. Though she did not do this unpleasantly as much as firmly, this development nonetheless irritated and/or amused my wife (depending on the nature and severity of the criticism). It was almost as though my mother-in-law felt her daughter creeping up on her, so to speak, and wished to reassert her authority. I watched this process with some detachment since I was happily exempt from criticism.

Indeed my mother-in-law became vastly more critical of life in general and especially of her long-deceased husband who had died in his sixties. She recounted his deficiencies in considerable and explicit (and, eventually, mind-numbing) detail. She also developed a hitherto suppressed sense of humor. When, in her last illness, she asked a nurse to get in touch with "my daughter," and the nurse asked which one, she replied, "Either one. They're both the same."

My mother-in-law kept her faculties to the end of her life, kept her grandchildren sorted out and accounted for, lived in her own home, and drove her ancient and ailing body tenaciously.

She thereby set a good example for those of us who were in the process of catching up.

Thinking about some of the implications of catching up, it occurred to me that a consolidation of generations is something worth considering. When children become "old," is it not sensible to consider living once more with parents as they did in childhood? Now the caring roles are reversed and a different kind of love and closeness becomes possible.

Certainly such reunions have potential difficulties and tensions. I have never tried such a relationship myself, but I have friends who have cared for elderly parents unto death and done so in a way that has added greatly to the lives of both generations. Of course, this is not a novel idea. It is the practice in many if not all "pre-modern" societies but I suspect that for most emancipated, middle-class Americans it is quite unthinkable. They treasure their "freedom" and "independence" and varied life-styles too much to take on such responsibility, and I know many grandparents who are equally independent and would as soon live with their "old children" as with Hottentots.

Part of the problem I suspect is that a kind of "internal civility" has vanished, a degree of courtesy and consideration within the household which is essential if generations are to inhabit the same space. With more Americans living longer, is it possible that "catching up" may come to have some larger social significance? Should not the old care for their own? I don't mean to pick on cruises but caring seems more human somehow than cruising.

LIFE ON HOLD

THE AGE OF TELECOMMUNICATIONS CERTAINLY HAS ITS DOWN SIDE.
The other day when some breezy young lady said: "This is the
XYZ Company. May I put you on hold?" I replied with some
asperity: "No, you may not. I am too old to spend the rest of
my life on hold."

That seemed to do it. "I'll put you through," she said,
doubtlessly turning to her next-desk neighbor and saying,
"There's an old nut on the line. I was afraid to keep him on
hold."

My columnist friend Wally Trabing wrote a great piece the
other day on such modern insolences as "May I say who's calling?" the implication being that you may not be important
enough for even a little bit of Mr. Officious's time. Or, equally
annoying, "May I ask what you wish to speak to Mr. Officious
about?" Again one has the feeling that what one has to say to
Mr. Officious may be judged by his secretary to be of insuffi-
cient significance to bother him.

I am reminded of Lily Tomlin's marvelous telephone oper-
ator on "Laugh In": "Is this the party to whom I am speaking?"

But there are more cosmic implications to being put on
hold. It seems to me that many, or perhaps most, Americans
put their lives on hold. It is one of my complaints about the
inhuman business of retirement. Millions of Americans forego

many of the small but rejuvenating pleasures of life until they're retired. How often has one heard a couple say they are looking forward to doing that, going there, whatever, when they have retired. It used to be said that Americans expected to live more fully in the lives of their children than in their own lives. They opted for "deferred gratification" rather than for more immediate satisfactions. Now the deferred gratifications are more often directed at the retirement years. Bad policy, in my view. First of all, you may retire and die. By deferring gratification you may indeed hasten your demise. Remember what some ancient sage said about "all work..."? I have always believed that sustained hard labor of whatever kind unleavened by fun, by joy and delight in daily life, by "time off" and by play (not, certainly, by jogging; that seems to me a grim and lonely form of penance for overeating, drinking, etc.) kills. And usually sooner rather than later. Retirement encourages the division of life into deadly hard work and belated leisure. Both, I am convinced, are bad for one's psychic and physical health. Leisure, I suspect, is almost as dangerous as hard work. At least it summons up for me the image of lolling on a Hawaiian beach à la Club Med and eating and drinking too much.

I am convinced that very few Americans have any idea of how to live. Some years ago, the Penny University gang spent several months' worth of our weekly sessions discussing how to live *a day*, twenty-four hours! It turned out to be a fascinating exercise. What we discovered was that *a day is a life!* We were talking not simply about a day but about how one lived his/her whole existence. I don't mean to be a nag but it seems to me to be the case that if you don't know how to live a day the odds aren't very good for the long haul. You may be taught elementary hygiene in high school and how to use condoms for safe sex, but that's about as far as it goes.

I have written before of the notion of living life backward in imagination from the hour of one's death in order to get things right. If you try that scheme the first (and most disheartening) thing you run into is *retirement*. With reasonable life-expectancy that's fifteen or twenty years, quite a chunk of time, before you get back to the serious business of making a living, marrying, raising children, etc. I suspect the typical American, starting at the other end, the youth end, only thinks as far forward as a job, profession or career. Since he or she has no real notion of "old" and cannot imagine becoming old, or, at least, being old, that part of life is simply a blank, something to be faced when you come to it. Something in your heart of hearts, in your innermost being, that you do not really think will happen. Or, if it does, it will be a time when you do all the things you've never had the time to do, a period of unabashed self-indulgence, a self-indulgence that you've *earned*. "Earned" is the determinative word here. How have you earned this bonanza of tours and cruises and whatnot? Well, by working your ass off to buy a house, to provide for the little woman (a rather outmoded notion, to be sure), by raising and educating the kids. By keeping your nose to the great American grindstone and your shoulder to the wheel. So what we're dealing with here is not one wholesome, integrated life but two rather casually related lives connected by retirement. Life before and after. Question: "Is there life after this one?" Answer: "Of course, that's why we have Social Security."

But that's obviously no way to live. The world is full of retired men (not so many women, as I have noted before) who are fighting valiantly to triumph over retirement. Many, of course, do, and are understandably proud of their accomplishment, but at the same time one senses that they are a little uneasy about it. It takes so much time and effort, so much planning and bustling about (and a good deal of money that might perhaps be better spent). It turns out unexpectedly that retirement is almost as much work as work itself. It may even require more imagination and energy than the old "nine to five."

What the young are able to observe about retirement in the persons of their parents and grandparents is not usually of a nature to encourage them to think well of that condition. I hear young friends say things like: "Dad has retired and is really handling it pretty well." That is to say, he hasn't lapsed into black depression or become an inveterate boozer.

It's time, I believe, to form the Society for the Prevention of Retirement. Whether one views retirement as a time when "you really start living," or a time when "you really start dying," it has to go, the sooner the better.

No more life on hold...

JOY AND LOVE
ARE THE ANSWERS

SURPRISED BY JOY

THE ANGLICAN THEOLOGIAN, C.S. LEWIS, WROTE A BOOK ENTITLED *Surprised by Joy.* The joy that surprised Lewis was his experience of being born again as a devout Christian. I thought of the title the other day when we received a Christmas card from a dear old friend. She is in her late seventies or early eighties and has had more than of her share of buffetings from life, among them a series of major operations and a husband with Alzheimer's. She wrote that, rather to her surprise, she found herself waking each morning with joy at the day that lay ahead.

I am, of course, much preoccupied by the changes that age brings with it: the surprises, some not particularly pleasant ones, others quite wonderful. Old age has its quite distinctive "ages" or phases if you will. I think it is characteristic of Americans generally to wish to force life, to make it conform to some preconceived plan or pattern, to hold it down, to throttle it until it yields what the individual desires from it. But that doesn't work for old age (if, indeed, it works for any age). Old age seems to be, above all else, a time when we let life *come to us,* so to speak. It is only thus that we can be "surprised by joy."

I have argued often that when we are young it is very difficult to think of being old. Or, more specifically, to imagine what being old consists of. I suppose I must have thought of old age when I was young but I cannot recall ever having thought of it in any comprehensive or positive way. It was associated in my mind with increasing physical limitations, with illness and disease and generally failing powers of perception and imagination. The matter of "imagining" old age rather puts me in mind of the heroism of a Congressional Medal of Honor winner in World War I from my hometown of Baltimore. George Redwood was a classic intellectual, shy and introspective. In the midst of near panic in his unit he had shown great courage and resourcefulness. While men of action failed dismally, he had been resolute. How did he explain his reaction, a newspaper reporter asked him? After a moment's reflection, Redwood answered that he had already imagined the worst that could happen and had armed himself to face it.

By the same token, if we in youth or middle age could enter imaginatively into the world of old age, we would be much better prepared to cope with it when, as it must, it overtakes us. And of course it is not simply a matter of coping, it is more an attitude of receptivity, a readiness to believe that old age can be a unique and remarkable time, a harvesting of all that has been planted earlier. "One is always at home in one's past," Vladimir Nabokov has written. And home, as we know, is where the heart is. So in old age we come home.

But joy? How can there be joy in the decaying flesh and the imminence of death? I do not know how. It is one of the surprises, one of the mysteries. An essential part of it, I suspect, is a deepening awareness of the extraordinary richness and complexity of life. A rhyme of Robert Louis Stevenson's sticks in my memory: "The world is so full of a number of things / I think we should all be as happy as kings." Leaving aside the obviously dubious proposition that kings are happy, one does feel as one grows older the marvelous intricacy of the world, its endless and inexplicable wonders. I suppose in part it is the fact that one has the time to reflect upon the multiformity of man- and womankind, and the splendor of history as the inexhaustible record of human hopes and strivings.

Many of the things that one took for granted in one's youth or middle years are in old age endowed with "the glows and glories and final illustrativeness which belong only to every real thing, and to real things only." For example, the whole process of having and raising children which my wife and I took more or less in stride without any particular reflection seems in retrospect quite an astonishing experience, and seeing our children in turn raising their children more astonishing still.

So it is with the extension of our own brief, if engrossing, histories back into our collective history, the story of the species. A modern theorist has proclaimed "the end of history" with the collapse of the Soviet Union and its "bloc." That seems to me quite silly. If history comes to an "end" it will be because we choose to forget it. It only exists, after all, in our memory and if we decide to expunge it, if we agree with James Joyce, that prophet of the modern consciousness, that "history is a nightmare from which we must awake," then we will surely lapse into that barbarism of which we see today so many anticipations.

Besides having history to instruct and delight us, we have nature to endlessly charm and heal us. Here again old age has a special relationship to nature. Perhaps because our days are more consciously numbered, the joys of nature seem ever richer and more abundant; what grows briefer grows dearer.

So I understand and admire (and share) our old friend's joy in life and know it to be one of those pleasant surprises of old age. If I had been inclined to forget, a letter from a reader would remind me. C.P. writes: "I have indeed come of age and what a glorious and magnificent feeling it is."

LOVE AND LET LOVE

PERHAPS IT IS AN ILLUSION, BUT I FIRMLY BELIEVE THAT THE PRINcipal consolation of old age is a deeper and richer sense of the meaning of love. That deeper, richer sense is a kind of compensation for one's physical diminishments, for aching joints and stiff sinews.

There is a good deal of glib, loose talk about love these days but, if we may judge by failed marriages and disintegrating relationships, there is not much of it in practical fact.

I suppose it is safe to say that the greatest words on love are to be found in St. Paul's first letter to the Corinthians: "Though I speak with the tongues of men and of angels and have not love, I am become as a sounding brass or a tinkling cymbal. And though I have the gift of prophecy, and understand all mysteries, and all knowledge; and though I have all faith, so that I could remove mountains, and have not love, I am nothing. And though I bestow all my goods to feed the poor, and though I give my body to be burned, and have not love, it profiteth me nothing. Love suffereth long, and is kind; love envieth not; love vaunteth not itself, is not puffed up, doth not behave itself unseemly, seeketh not her own, is not easily provoked, thinketh no evil: rejoiceth not in iniquity, but rejoiceth in the truth beareth all things, believeth all things, hopeth all things, endureth all things." Including old age. Or especially old age.

Love is not, of course, physical desire (although it may include that emotion); love is the surrender of self to another and that surrender is made up of innumerable acts of surrender of self over time, over a lifetime. In 1793 William Manning, a semi-literate Massachusetts farmer, wrote: "[Man] has so strongly implanted in him a desire of Selfe Seporte, Selfe Defence, Selfe Love, Selfe Conceit, Selfe Importance, & Selfe Aggrandizement, that it Ingroses all his care and attention so that he can see nothing beyond Selfe."

Though Manning does not say so, we know that the only way out of the prison of self is through love. Above all, we know that love is not easy because even pitifully small renunciations of self commonly come hard. In our modern-day obsession with our rights, they come even harder. In this era, our first response to most of life's dilemmas is to loudly proclaim *our* rights. That is certainly a natural and often an entirely appropriate initial reaction when we feel that we have been treated unjustly, but it is not a particularly happy frame of mind to get into because it places us and our wounded egos at the center of our consciousness and thereby diverts us from those unselfish, sacrificial acts that make it possible for us to give and receive love. Can't we state this as the most basic natural or moral law of the universe? That we can't live without love, that none of us can *deserve* love as much as we need it and that we cannot have it without sacrifice of self? Is there anything plainer underneath the sun?

Can love have laws? What are the laws of love?

Well, one law is that infinitely difficult, virtually impossible (except for the saints) sacrifice of self. Lovers, if they are true lovers, have to practice that demanding discipline. Above all, parents have to sacrifice for their children. We expect that. Parents who are unwilling to make substantial sacrifices for their children appear to us as unnatural parents. The fact is that parenthood catches most of us quite unprepared. It often seems we are barely out of diapers before we are expected to assume the awesome responsibilities of parents. If our own parents have not loved and sacrificed for us, how are we to know how to care for our own often unbidden offspring who arrive with virtually infinite demands upon us? Fortunately, like most members of the animal kingdom, our natural instincts bond us with our children and so teach us, willy-nilly, the sacrificial nature of love. But the lesson is by no means necessarily extended to our fellow creatures.

Frederick Nietzsche wrote that we are "only creative in the shadow of love and love's illusions." That might be a second law of love. We have to love the task to simply do it well (which simply means whole-heartedly).

It helps to love the natural world, but that may be the easiest love of all because it seldom requires sacrifice and it is sometimes a refuge for those who find it too demanding to love other human beings. Loving animals is a good way to begin to learn the discipline of loving, because animals, being wholly dependent on us, have to be cared for in at least modestly unselfish ways.

And what has all this to do with old age? It seems to me that many old people—certainly not all—have learned the meaning of love through lifetimes of sacrificial acts, through extended networks of loving connections to children, grandchildren, brothers, sisters, cousins, dear old friends. As time burns the dross of life away, the truly important things, as opposed to transient and ephemeral things, can be seen more clearly, and we know, if we did not know before, that love is the most important and the most enduring thing of all and that knowledge strengthens us and sustains us in the wearing away of the flesh. That is or should be our legacy. Through living we have learned the primacy of love.

Robert Browning's "Love Among the Ruins" ends:

Oh heart! oh blood that freezes, blood that burns!
Earth returns
For whole centuries of folly, noise and sin!
Shut them in
With their triumphs and their glories and the rest
Love is best.

Old age knows that.

✳

The Crossing Press
publishes a full selection of
titles of general interest.
To receive our current catalog,
please call toll-free,
800-777-1048.
